OP 43   25—

IO

Trial & Error
& the Idea
of Progress

Madsen Pirie

Trial & Error & the Idea of Progress

Open Court
LaSalle & London

Copyright © Open Court Publishing Company 1978

All rights reserved for all countries. No part of this book may be reproduced by any means without the written permission of the publisher, Open Court Publishing Company, La Salle, Illinois.

Printed in the United States of America

Library of Congress Cataloging in Publication Data

Pirie, Madsen, 1940 –
   Trial and error and the idea of progress.

   Includes bibliographical references.
   1. Progress. I. Title.
HM101.P53   301.24   77-8577
ISBN 0-87548-344-5

To Norman and Dorothy Gash

Contents

Preface ix
Chapter 1: The Idea of Progress 1
Chapter 2: Aims and Methods in Science 15
Chapter 3: A New Demarcation 49
Chapter 4: The Acquisition and Improvement of Skills 67
Chapter 5: History and the Study of Mankind 85
Chapter 6: Objectives in Society 105
Chapter 7: Progress in Economic Life 123
Chapter 8: Testing and Social Progress 157
Chapter 9: Optimum Conditions 191
Conclusion 209
Bibliography 213
Index 219

Preface

This book is the product of work done towards my doctorate at the University of St. Andrews. My greatest debt is to my supervisor, Bernard Mayo, professor of Moral Philosophy at St. Andrews. I owe much to my first teacher of philosophy, H. B. Acton, whose death in 1974 was a sad loss to scholarship.

Eamonn Butler, John Hutchinson, Helgi Juliusson, and Basil Purdue helped me considerably when I was first developing the ideas contained in this book. I acknowledge my debt to them now. My grateful thanks for assistance given at various times also go to Stuart Butler, André Carus, Linda Jones, Milla Osborne, and Kenneth and Eugenie Walden.

To the staff of Open Court I extend my special gratitude, especially to M. Blouke Carus, Thomas G. Anderson, and Dale E. Howard. Finally, but not least in importance, I wish to thank the source of this book: St. Andrews, the University and the City.

I
The Idea of Progress

This book is about progress and the methods used to achieve it. It explores the meaning of progress, its constituent elements, and the conditions which favor it. It differs from previous works under similar titles[1] by confining itself to analysis rather than evaluation. Instead of appealing to collective standards in order to categorize changes as either good or bad, I have tried to weave a thread through a variety of human activities, concentrating on the methods by which people come closer to the achievement of their aims. In doing so, I have reasserted the importance of man's motives and intentions in his relationship with his circumstances. In unifying the idea of progress through a variety of different disciplines and activities, I have attempted to show how men and women embark upon creative procedures which converge on the satisfaction of their objectives.

J. H. Plumb talks (in "The Historian's Dilemma," 1964) of "one certain judgement of value that can be made about history, and that is *the idea of progress*. If this great human truth were once more to be frankly accepted," he tells us, "the reason for it, and the consequences of it, consistently and imaginatively explored and taught, history would not only be an infinitely richer education but also play a much more effective part in the culture of western society."[2] Unfortunately, he neither tells us what it is, how we can recognize it, nor how we can be sure that it is what it seems to be. We are given to understand, though, that it is something good. Arnold Beichman[3] describes the derivatives of the word *progress* as "halo words," whose only function is to transform the words next to them by imparting a warm glow of approval. Thus while *violence* might be bad, *progressive violence* can be taken as good.

It is an instructive starting point in analysis to consider what the word *progress* actually means. Dictionaries define it in terms of "forward or onward movement," "advance," "improvement," "satisfactory development," and so on. It strikes the attention immediately that these are all words or phrases which imply a standard of measurement. Movement in a forward or onward direction requires that we know which direction is forward. *Advance* is meaningless unless one is advancing toward something. *Improvement,* meaning "better than before," must necessarily involve the question "better in what respects?" The notion of satisfactory development carries the implication that there is something to be satisfied. All of them, we might say, are *aim related*. All of them implicitly convey the notion of an aim which is required to be achieved. Movement or development can be regarded as progress if it is in the direction of the achievement of that aim. The notion of progress only becomes intelligible in terms of the aim or aims whose fulfillment is required. There is no such thing as progress in the abstract—only progress toward whatever aim or aims are under consideration.

When Plumb (and others) talk of progress in history, our first step in understanding the term is to inspect the implicit aims which must necessarily be involved. Only after the aims have been identified will we be in any position to see whether there has been any movement in the direction of their fulfillment. The person who talks of "human progress" must always be using the term to mean advancement toward particular and identifiable aims. If we do not know what they are, there can be no way of either assenting to, or denying, the validity of his claim.

If everyone shared the same aims, and accorded them the same relative priorities, we could all agree quite happily on what would be constituted by progress, even though we might disagree on whether in fact any particular development had led closer to the achievement of those ends. Unfortunately for simplicity, there is no such agreement. Not only do we disagree on the facts of individual developments, we also disagree over the aims which we are measuring. Two people might agree that a particular state actually brought about an increased ability to fulfill an aim, but they might not agree on the desirability of the aim; they might not share it. If people hold contradictory aims, then one man's progress will be another man's retrogression; for the same development will take one man nearer his aim, while taking his rival further from an aim which lies in the opposite direction.

Use of the term *progress* thus implies movement in the direction of an aim which is shared and approved by the user of the term. When people talk generally of progress, they are speaking of movement toward aims which they too partake of. A speaker who invites the agreement of his audience to the assertion that there has been progress is inviting them to assent to two things: firstly, that there has indeed been movement toward an objective and, secondly, that this objective is regarded by the audience as desirable. They could withhold their agreement on either of the two counts. In the quotation above, Plumb is asking us to "frankly accept" the "great human truth" of progress in history. He is thus asking us to assent, firstly, to his aims and, secondly, to his contention that history has brought us nearer the achievement of them.

The sad fact for those who would have us gird up our loins

for a great crusade of progress is that this agreement over human aims is nowhere to be found. Not only do people find themselves possessed of differing motivations, they illustrate this fact by passing contradictory judgments on various human developments. By no means will everyone concur with the suggestion that the Industrial Revolution brought progress. They might, it is true, concede that it brought some people nearer the fulfillment of their aims, but they will dispute the progress by disputing the validity of the aims. To those who nominate increased material prosperity as a high-order aim, the Industrial Revolution is seen as definite progress. To those who value, instead, such things as the "measured rhythm of rural life" or man's contentment with his lot, that same Industrial Revolution is seen as representing a retrograde step. In any consideration of progress, therefore, we must not fail to take account of the aim-related nature of judgments which concern it.

Despite this subjectivity, though, there are some fields in which there is universal agreement that progress has been made. The natural sciences, for example, seem to have enjoyed a striking and unparalleled success since the time of Newton. During a period in which it has seemed to many observers that in fields such as morality, philosophy, and politics man has covered and re-covered the old ground many times over, the natural sciences have appeared to march forward in constant and linear progress, with confident strides. Whereas in other subjects people are still debating and disputing the essentials of their disciplines, in science, at least, it seems that there is near-universal acceptance of what constitutes the fundamentals of the activity. Thus it is that science has appeared to move on from one problem to the next, making every step look like a forward one. Nor would many dispute that there has been progress in athletic attainment. There is little doubt that many men today can run farther and faster, jump higher, swim more rapidly, and throw the discus, javelin, and shot for greater distances than their predecessors. Since these things started to be measured accurately, the graph of scientific and athletic performance can be drawn as an upward curve.

The first question to be considered, then, is why there should be admitted progress in some fields but not in others. Why is it that we can all agree to describe the attainments in science and athletic activity as "progress"? Thomas Kuhn poses the question in his *Structure of Scientific Revolutions:* "Why should the enterprise sketched above [science] move steadily ahead in ways that, say, art, political theory, or philosophy does not? Why is progress a perquisite reserved almost exclusively for the activities we call science?"[4] Kuhn partly answers his question. He asks us to "notice immediately that part of the question is entirely semantic," and advances the thesis that "to a very great extent the term 'science' is reserved for fields that do progress in obvious ways."[5] If Kuhn is right, then the problem of progress becomes the problem of science. To say that we call whatever makes progress by the name of "science" is to say nothing about progress.

The contention in this book is that Kuhn's answer is inadequate; that there is something special about scientific activity which enables us to agree upon what constitutes progress within it. The search for the fundamentals of progress starts with a close examination of what it is that constitutes scientific activity, and the task is to isolate the constituent elements of progress in science.

The "trial and error" in my title is a tribute to Sir Karl Popper, whose method of "conjecture and refutation"[6] has solved the problem of induction.[7] Although the view of science which I advance is a considerable modification of Popper's system in many key fundamentals, the Popper method is taken as the starting point for criticism and alteration in both method and conception. Retained throughout my account, however, is the basic "trial and error" element which Popper formulated. Despite the fact that my conclusions lead me to propose that we are not proposing what Popper thinks we are proposing, nor testing for what he thinks we are testing for, nor even attempting to achieve by the activity what Popper thinks we should be achieving, there remains (at the end of the analysis) the notion of the elimination of variously proposed alternatives, rather than the computation of necessary steps.

The central problem is seen as the minimization of the use of nonconclusive arguments, and establishing the importance of testing. The proposition "All A is B" necessarily implies "This A is B," meaning that it would be impossible for the first to be true, but not the second. The argument is conclusive. But the proposition "This A is B" does not, of course, imply that "All A is B." It may be taken as slight evidence toward it, in the absence of knowledge about any A that is not B, and the more As which are found to be also Bs, then the more do we regard them as evidence supporting the proposition "All A is B." Nonetheless, the argument is inconclusive, and, however many As we find that are Bs, it is quite possible that there are undiscovered As which are not Bs. It is the inductive style of argument which proceeds in this way from the particular to the general.

Popper has provided us with an alternative whereby the generalization is proposed by an imaginative leap, and then tested by its deducible consequences. In this book it is argued that these imaginative leaps must be seen as relating to some purpose, and that while their proposals can never finally be established in any way, they can be retained so long as they serve that purpose better than their rivals, and rejected whenever a rival proposal is found to serve that purpose even better. The function of testing is seen as determining which of various competing proposals best serves the particular purpose in question.

Trial and Error and the Idea of Progress represents an attempt to abstract from a consideration of scientific activity a formula whose application enables progress to be made, and an attempt to apply this formula to other fields of human endeavor in order to investigate the possibility of meaningful discussion of progress within them. Finally, it is an attempt to postulate those conditions which are within the control of society and which can be manipulated in such a way as to create a climate favorable to the making of progress.

On the question of evaluation of preferences, no attempt is made herein to suggest that some human aims are more worthy than others, or why they should be considered so. Where the term *progress* is used, it is used in a way which does not carry the value judgments necessary for the everyday use of the term. *Progress,* in this work, is taken to refer to the closer achievement of ends, *whatever those ends might be.* It is taken as an avowedly aim-related term, and is used only with reference to an end. *Progress* is used to mean "progress toward something," and the value of that something is not relevant to the analysis and discussion with which I am concerned. It could be explained by saying that progress is considered here only as devoid of content: this discussion is only with the achievement of aims (or with the closer approach to such achievement). A discussion of which ends *ought* to be achieved represents a completely different approach, and the use of arguments of a totally different order from those encountered herein. I deal here with the *structure* of progress, not its content.

One of the major conclusions of this work is that the principles of progress (abstracted from scientific activity) form a unifying theme which underlies the attempt to achieve human aims in any activity. The concepts which in science emerge as "models" and "model testing"[8] are broadened to the concepts of "attempts" and "attempt testing," and are susceptible of application in any field in which we engage in activity directed toward bringing us nearer our objectives. The formula which shows what is necessary before progress can be made is posited not as a recommendation but as a description of how progress is actually made.

The analysis of progress in scientific activity[9] is followed by a consideration of untestable imaginative leaps.[10] I propose that the most valid demarcation between propositions consists in their separation into those which can assist us in progressing toward objectives and those which cannot. If testing and consequent choice are vital ingredients of progress, then my claim is that no choice can be made between untestable propositions and, consequently, no progress can be made with them toward an objective.

An inspection of the study of history and the social sciences is undertaken[11] to establish whether the peculiar limitations imposed by the subject matter of these disciplines in any way limit the application of the method of progress abstracted from science. The field of human skills and their acquisition[12] is examined to see whether the application of "knowledge how," rather than "knowledge that,"[13] involves any necessary restriction on the validity of the elements of progress in them and their related activities. Only after analysis of the different types of activities humans engage in, and of the types of motivations to which they are subject, is there consideration of progress in social and political fields.[14]

It is not quite a tautology to say that if progress means the closer approach to our aims, we must desire progress if we desire our aims. What saves us from tautology is the fact that we have a hierarchy of aims, with lower objectives serving higher ones. Cases can arise in which we find ourselves "satisfied" by what appears to be only the partial fulfillment of an objective. These are cases in which we have achieved the higher end, which we thought the lower objective was serving, not realizing that complete achievement of the lower objective would *not* serve the higher end. It is not tautological to say that the desire to achieve our ends can always be assumed,

Trial and Error

because there are some ends which we hold without realizing that they do not serve the higher ends which we think they do. There are undoubtedly, too, some aims which we hold unconsciously, being unaware, with the thinking part of our minds, of what our desires really are. The progress we make toward our higher and our unconscious ends is also discussed[15] before there is any consideration of the progress of man in his societies.

The judgment that certain types of social organization are more conducive than others to efficient progress toward our objectives derives from an investigation into progress which man has actually made, and analysis of how it is made. Despite the absence of recommendations, there are clear overtones to the book which might provide lessons for man and society. From analysis and interpretation emerge conditional proposals which suggest that *if* we wish to achieve certain states, *then* we can take specified steps to bring about those states. To those who might wish to achieve these aforementioned states, the argument might propose a program of positive action (or at least provide the outlines of one).

The idea of progress on any general scale is, apart from sporadic instances, relatively modern. Individual progress is, of course, a very old idea indeed. Even in primitive societies there existed the notion of bettering one's lot in life, of improving one's skills, and of moving toward the achievement of limited objectives. But only rarely, before the Renaissance, was there the general view that the world might be becoming a better place for everyone. Some Romans viewed the extension of their domain as progress toward the civilizing of mankind; some Christians viewed the march of the Christian religion as progress toward peace and justice on earth. For only a few hundred years has there been the widespread view that man, with reasonable management, could hope to look to a future of ever-increasing satisfaction of his desires, and ever-increasing conquests of the sources of unhappiness.

If Kuhn is wrong to suggest that the term *science* is reserved for fields in which obvious progress is made, he is right to draw, as others have drawn, a close connection between science and progress. It is only with the rise of science in modern Europe that the idea of continuous progress in human history has come into its own. It is not so much the direct progress of science which has shown progress to be possible but, rather, the technology arising from scientific progress which has given force to man's desires. Technology is not an end, but a means which can be applied to a variety of ends. The rise of science in Europe has brought an attendant technology capable of fulfilling objectives in many spheres. That technology has been used to increase material prosperity, to bring a wide range of consumer goods within reach of the average citizen; it has been used to make travel safer and faster, to extend communication; it has been used to reduce drudgery and disease, and to bring opportunities and the leisure to indulge them to the common man. Everywhere technology has been seen as the strength in man's elbow, as the force which turns desire into reality.

Technology has brought frightening dimensions to war and accidents as well. It is morally neutral, merely a force to be harnessed to whatever motives man applies. Whatever man has wanted to do, both good and evil, technology has enabled him to do it more effectively. Moreover, technology has been thought of as limitless: whatever force is needed to solve whatever problem, technology has been seen as capable of applying infinite support. One definition of a sophisticated modern economy[16] involves the notion that resources can be directed toward achievement of almost any desire—even a flight to the moon.

The growth of scientifically based technology can be seen as the chief spur to the modern idea of progress. If progress means that one is able to approach nearer the achievement of objectives, and technology is the method used to bring this about, then the connection is self-evident.

But we cannot assume that it is only material desires which technology has enabled us to fulfill more adequately. The technological progress which started in Western Europe has been harnessed to nonmaterial desires. By performing necessary work, it increases leisure time; by promoting economic growth, it enables more resources to be committed to such things as education. The optimism which has prevailed over such a large part of the time since the rise of scientific technology has been substantially due to the view that man would be able to apply that technology toward ever-increasing satisfaction of his desires.[17] For the greater portion of that time it was an optimism which has been justified.

The modern view, which certainly prevailed until well into the present century,[18] and which is still probably the most widespread view, is that each generation of man will inhabit a world in which the general conditions of life will be better than they were for the previous generation. This is the central fact about the idea of progress which has ruled for several hundred years. Progress has been seen as inevitable; and while temporary setbacks may have shaken this view, none has dispelled it.

The theme of this work is that progress is not something necessary and inevitable, like the "self-sustaining economic growth" of W. W. Rostow's model.[19] It is, rather, the result of deliberate application by man, the fruits of a determination backed by a valid technique. The clear implications are that there are conditions appropriate to efficient and successful progress, and that there are conditions under which progress will be slow and difficult. It is perhaps appropriate that, after the idea of progress has enjoyed so long a run, an analysis should be undertaken of its component elements and of the circumstances under which it proceeds smoothly.

In view of the close connection between the modern idea of progress and the rise of science and scientifically based technology, it is perhaps inevitable that an inquiry into progress should begin with an examination of the methods of science.

Notes

[1] For example, J. B. Bury, *The Idea of Progress* (1920); Charles Van Doren, *The Idea of Progress* (1967); Sidney Pollard, *The Idea of Progress* (1968).

[2] J. H. Plumb, "The Historian's Dilemma" (1964).

[3] Arnold Beichman, *Nine Lies about America* (1972).

[4] Thomas S. Kuhn, *The Structure of Scientific Revolutions* (1962), ch. XIII.

[5] Ibid.

[6] Popper's shorthand description of the method of scientific inquiry. The phrase occurs in his book *Conjectures and Refutations* (1963), ch. 1: "Science: Conjectures and Refutations." Popper subsequently prefers the phrase "trial and error-elimination" in his *Objective Knowledge* (1972).

[7] The description of the problem and its solution first appeared in Popper's *Logik der Forschung* (1934), a modified version of which was published as *The Logic of Scientific Discovery* (1959).

[8] Ch. 2, below.

[9] Ibid.

[10] Ch. 3, below.

[11] Ch. 5, below.

[12] Ch. 4, below.

[13] A distinction drawn by Gilbert Ryle in *The Concept of Mind* (1949), ch. II.

[14] Chs. 7 and 8, below.

[15] Ch. 6, below.

[16] This is the kernel of W. W. Rostow's definition in *The Stages of Economic Growth* (1960).

[17] The significance of Aldous Huxley's *Brave New World* (1932) lies in its being the first novel to project an unpleasant technological future state. The first novel to present technology allied to unpleasant consequences was probably Mary Wollstonecraft's *Frankenstein*.

[18] Only during the past decade has the idea emerged that pollution and environmental damage might outweigh the gains of technological advance and economic growth.

[19] In *The Stages of Economic Growth* W. W. Rostow advances the idea that a stage is reached in the growth of a modern economy at which the return achieved is sufficient to maintain and increase the rate of expansion. When capital growth occurs at such a rate that the "lead sector industry" can no longer absorb it, it floods over into other industries, promoting an expansionist surge in them, too.

2
Aims & Methods in Science

The Popper account of scientific method[1] is not without its weaknesses, the central one being the very notion of "falsification." Popper includes among his aims that of saving reality. "I propose to accept realism," he tells us, "as the only sensible hypothesis—as a conjecture to which no sensible alternative has ever been offered."[2] He spells it out in a later passage: "Our main concern in philosophy and in science should be the search for truth," and goes on to say: "I accept the commonsense theory (defended and refined by Alfred Tarski) that truth is correspondence with the facts (or with reality); or, more precisely, that a theory is true if and only if it corresponds to the facts."[3]

It is because Popper thinks that "in science we search for truth"[4] that his terms are those which describe an objective reality. The search, he says, is for *verisimilitude,* or greatest truth content with lowest falsity content, and our competitive search for verisimilitude turns, "especially from the empirical point of view, into a competitive comparison of falsity contents."[5] He points out that

> we can never make absolutely certain that our theory is not lost. All we can do is to search for the falsity content

of our best theory. We do so by trying to refute our theory; that is, by trying to test it severely in the light of all our objective knowledge and all our ingenuity. It is, of course, always possible that the theory may be false even if it passes all these tests; this is allowed for by our search for verisimilitude. *But if it passes all these tests then we may have good reason to conjecture that our theory, which as we know has a greater truth content than its predecessor, may have no greater falsity content.* And if we fail to refute the new theory, especially in fields in which its predecessor has been refuted, then we can claim this as one of the objective reasons for *the conjecture that the new theory is a better approximation to truth than the old theory.*[6]

It is worth quoting Popper at some length on this point to establish quite clearly that he regards scientific theories as conjectures concerning the state of reality. They are, he tells us, either true or false. Either the facts are like that or they are not. And while we have no way of knowing which theories are true, we can hope to show which are false. Popper says that whereas we have no criterion of truth, we do have a partial criterion of falsity.[7] No experiment, or series of experiments, will ever show us that a theory is true, but if we could find a single counterexample, then we would be entitled to say that the theory was false.

The weakness in the falsification approach is contained within the "if" of the clause "if we could find a counterexample." For us to be able to declare a theory false, we would need to be certain that we had indeed found a counterexample. It is all very well to talk in terms of testing "severely in the light of all our objective knowledge," but whence comes this objective knowledge? As Lakatos has shown, we cannot have it both ways.[8] If no knowledge is ever certain, there can be no certain objective knowledge against which a new theory may be tested. Whenever we make any scientific test, we do so by

Trial and Error

assuming some of our background knowledge to be unproblematic. It may be an assumption of the trivial form "that our senses are not deceiving us" or it may be of a more complicated nature, such as "the laws of electromagnetic radiation continue to hold for a previously unexplored area of physics." Neither assumption can be conclusively justified.

Since all of our experiments depend upon the results of other experiments to provide the stable background for testing, we are left with a circular process in which our scientific "knowledge" may be seen as a self-contained system. It may be convenient to accept the commonsense hypothesis that this self-contained system describes reality, but it seems unfortunate that a rationalist methodology, designed at least in part to save reality, should do so only by what amounts to an initial act of faith. Since our interpretation of what we conjecture are accurately observed results depends upon previous interpretation of what we previously conjectured were accurately observed results, there is no breakout from the system into any kind of objectivity, no point at which the chain is anchored to an objective reality.

It may well be that "sensible alternatives" are difficult to conjecture. Since our experiments are judged for results against the background of assumed knowledge, we build up a body of scientific conjecture in which internal consistency is at a premium. It is not, says Lakatos, that we perform our test and the universe shouts *"no";* rather is it a case of our performing our test and the universe shouting *"inconsistent."*[9] We might thus be led to propose that *either* our body of scientific hypotheses does indeed "correspond with the facts" *or* that the universe is deceiving us in a systematic way. But there remains a third possibility, which is that there might be other systems, different from the body of interpretation which we have built up, but possessing internal consistency to the same degree as that of our present system.

The realization that, when we test, we cannot assume "the light of all our objective knowledge" means that we cannot say in the event of a discrepancy that we have successfully shown the proposition under test to be false. And out of the same window as goes falsification must also depart the idea of greater verisimilitude. If we cannot, for certain, reject what is false, neither can we accumulate hypotheses of greater truth content, and neither can we talk any longer of greater correspondence with the facts. When we test, we are testing a conjunction of the hypothesis with what we think we already know. "What we think we already know" is no more than those propositions which testing has not led us to abandon.

If the search is for "inconsistency content" rather than "falsity content," we may see how it could come about that, starting with different interpretations and assumptions, we could, in theory, build up a body of consistent "knowledge" different from the body of knowledge we have actually built up, given the interpretations and assumptions we started with. In plainer terms, if the self-consistent and circular system is tied at no point to an objective reality, we can envisage many equivalent, but different, systems which we might have arrived at instead of our present system. In what sense, then, does our scientific knowledge correspond with the facts?

Science as a human discipline appears to have made widely accepted progress, despite the absence of any firm link tying its propositions to an objective reality. Perhaps scientific conjectures, while not purporting to describe reality, do something which we can regard as equally acceptable. If it is sensible to talk of an objective reality, it is equally sensible to appreciate that, because we are dependent upon our senses and our minds for an interpretation of it, there will be a "form of reality" appropriate to us as observers. That is, there will be a form in which reality cannot but seem to be presented to us because of the nature of our sensory and mental equipment. We may imagine that other beings with different senses and different types

Trial and Error

of minds will have their own "form of reality" in the way in which objective reality cannot but be interpreted by them. We are speaking here not only of those aspects of the universe already contemplated by man, but those which are capable of such contemplation. The form of reality is thus seen as a potential, not necessarily an actual, appreciation. It may be thought of as the total description of the universe from the point of view of the mind and senses of any particular species. It is, moreover, the only reality which is (by definition) appreciable by that species.

If the human race were to disappear suddenly, then its form of reality would not disappear with it. It would remain as a potential way of understanding the universe, to be realized at such a time as a new species emerged with the same type of sense organs and minds as humans possess. But when we talk of "reality" and our attempts to understand it, we are talking of the form in which any objective reality is accessible to our contemplation. It is a reality which already has the pattern of man stamped on it. There is no point at all in attempting to concern ourselves with the objective reality which presents that particular form to us, since (by definition) it is a reality forever beyond our detection or comprehension.

But even this "form of reality," this aspect of existence as it can only be observed and interpreted by man, is not tied logically to the world of our scientific propositions. We have no way of ascribing certain falsity to conjectures which are concerned with the universe of our observation, for either our senses may be deceiving us or the "stable knowledge" against which the conjectures are tested may itself be in error. One solution to this dilemma is to opt for a correspondence between scientific theories and the observed universe because "the overwhelming weight of common sense" supports such an identification. If the alternative is to believe that the universe is deceiving us in a systematic way, the temptation is great to believe, instead, that "inconsistency" can be equated with "falsity." The notion of "belief" is, however, a dangerous one.[10] In answer to Hume's problem of induction, many people, especially scientists, were prepared to say that the entire scientific system rested on the irrational belief that there is a logical connection between repeated instances of an event, the belief that what happened yesterday provided a reason for us to believe it would happen again tomorrow.

It was a desire to preserve induction which led to the inclusion of belief to supply the missing link, just as it is the desire to save reality which brings belief into this equation. Just as it proved possible to abandon induction and replace it with an acceptable alternative, thereby disposing of the "problem of induction," so it might be possible to get rid of the notion that scientific conjectures are purported descriptions of the observed universe, and yet replace it by an acceptable substitute.

The human race has access to devices other than description in its attempts to understand and to interpret. One such device is the *model,* or *analogue.* In circumstances where the real thing is for some reason denied us, we can proceed to extend our knowledge by the construction of a model. We can perform operations on the model which perhaps we could never perform on the real thing, and thereby gain greater understanding of whatever it is that our model is intended to represent. If the purpose of our scientific conjectures is to enable us to understand and to interpret, in some way, the observed universe, we can see that it is not necessary to regard them as putative descriptions of reality: we could propose instead that they bear more of the characteristics of a system of analogues.

What is suggested here is that scientists, despite the appearances of terminology, are not putting forward propositions which purport to describe the observed reality, but that they are, instead, proposing models whose function is to help us in some way interpret the observed reality. In other words, instead of saying, "I conjecture that, in our observed reality, all bodies attract each other with a force that varies inversely with the square of the distance between them," the scientist is saying, "I propose that, in order to understand our observed reality, we should contemplate a mental model of it in which bodies attract each other with a force that varies inversely with the square of the distance between them." While the two ways of putting it seem very similar, there are, nonetheless, fundamental implicit differences.

The differences with which we are here concerned are twofold. In the first place, the second approach makes it quite clear that the world of science is man-made. While the first way of putting things might lead to the impression that scientific activity consists in discovering, little by little, what already exists objectively, the second way clearly implies that science is created by man to serve his purposes. Scientific theories are not discovered, they are created, and scientific activity consists not in gaining access to an ever larger share of information waiting to be discovered, but in inventing ever more wide-ranging and sophisticated models in order to bring the observed universe within the ambit of our comprehension.

The second key difference, from our point of view, is that while the first approach involves us in the formulations of propositions which are either true or false, the second way of looking at scientific activity involves us in the proposal of models which are either good or bad. If we are dealing with propositions which purport to concern themselves with reality, with "the facts," then we encounter all the objections deriving from our inability to break out of the closed chain of internal consistency. Because all of our knowledge is dependent upon our other knowledge, we have no way of establishing any scientific proposition as definitely false, any more than we have of establishing it to be definitely true.

Once we realize, however, that we are talking about a system of analogues rather than a collection of propositions describing reality, the problem does not arise. We can now legitimately admit into our scientific activity the very conventionalism that Popper is so anxious to avoid.[11] We can say not that we falsify conjectures but that we *reject* proposed models which we find inadequate. We are not now asking if our scientific proposals have greater verisimilitude, or truth content with lower falsity content, than their predecessors; we are asking whether they serve our purposes better than their predecessors did. Before we enter the discussion as to what those purposes are, it is perhaps well to note that even the Lakatos modification of Popper involves the introduction of an explicit conventionalism into the system. When Lakatos points out that every test is in fact the testing of a conjunction of a new hypothesis and "unproblematic" background knowledge, he explains that the decision as to which knowledge is "unproblematic" is a conventional one.[12] If a discrepancy occurs in testing, the decision to cast doubt on the new theory is a conventional one. *We decide* which part of our knowledge shall be deemed as above suspicion.

This modification by Lakatos is major, and all of his careful attention to the actual procedures adopted by scientists in their research programs cannot alter the fact that the modification disposes of Popper's hope for an objective standard to which his system might be anchored. Lakatos attempts to devise rules whereby scientists can automatically know which information is suspect in the event of testing discrepancies, but since the rules amount to no more than a convenience, the way is wide open for any scientist to reject them. One of Lakatos's major concerns is to prevent situations arising in which new theories may be discarded because of undetected flaws in the background knowledge used in their testing. He instances the atomic theory of Prout (that the atomic weights of chemical elements are whole numbers),[13] and points out that when even the most accurate practical measure showed chlorine to have an atomic weight of 35.5, the theory was discarded. We know now, of course, since the idea

Trial and Error

of isotopes was introduced, that chlorine consists of two types (atomic weights 35 and 36) which give an *average* atomic weight of 35.5, and we can appreciate that the theory would not have been discarded had this been known at the time of testing.

The trouble with the Lakatos rules is that in saving the odd theory, like that of Prout, he compels us to retain many theories that are worthy of rejection. The whole process of scientific discovery would be slowed down considerably if scientists were to adopt in practice the maxims which Lakatos proposes in theory. Fortunately for science, they do not adopt such maxims. What scientists do in practice is to proceed as before, discarding theories which fail to survive critical tests, even including such theories as Prout's. If, with the tares, a few ears of wheat are also thrown away, science can always backtrack briefly at such a time as the pile-up of anomalies compels them to doubt the background knowledge that is used to reject some of these theories. This is precisely what happened in the case of Prout's theory. It *was* discarded, and it *was* subsequently rehabilitated as anomalies revealed a flaw in the narrow conception of a chemical element.

Perhaps fortunately for science, scientists are often committed to their theories in a highly personal way. As Kuhn[14] and others have observed, scientific progress is made more by new scientists concentrating on new issues than by old ones admitting that their ideas were wrong. Even though scientific activity proceeds at full speed, ruthlessly rejecting theories (like Prout's) which do not survive severe testing, some scientists are always sufficiently committed to the discarded theories to explore the possibility that the decision might have been unwise.

Lakatos has overlooked that one of the aims of science takes into account the rate of progress. We want knowledge, and *we want it now*. Under the Lakatos rules, progress would undoubtedly be made, safely and steadily. Under the system actually used by science (in a much more cavalier approach), progress is made quickly. Science can proceed, make mistakes, backtrack, pick up needlessly discarded theories, and still be years ahead of the point it would have reached with the painstaking approach of Lakatos. Lakatos, despite his introduction of conventional decisions, fails to take sufficient account of the aims of the activity.

If we regard scientific theories not as putative descriptions of reality but as proposed models, then the problem is easily solved. Scientists are asked not to ascribe truth or falsity to conjectures but to accept or to reject them as good or bad models. The conventionalism here is explicit and necessary. Unlike the conventionalism introduced by Lakatos into the simple Popper system, which was proposed as an unfortunate but unavoidable departure from objectivism, the conventionalism in the analogue system derives from a recognition that scientific activity is directed to the fulfillment of a human purpose. It ceases to be a question of "But is the universe like that?" and becomes instead a question of "But do we *want* that?"

The question of what is, or is not, a good model depends upon the whole purpose of the activity. Men do not engage in scientific activity aimlessly; nor do they choose it as a pleasant way of occupying themselves in order to pass the time. They engage in scientific activity to gain knowledge and understanding of the observed universe.[15] That knowledge and understanding are measured in terms of their ability to predict future events and to explain past ones. One can be said to have an effective grasp of the fundamental workings of a system if one is able to predict successfully the future outcomes of that system, and to "retrodict" the past outcomes. The question of why men should wish to be able to predict the behavior of the observed universe is not strictly relevant, provided that one accepts that they do; but it may assist that acceptance if one realizes that to *predict* is but one step short of to *control*. It

Trial and Error

may well be that man, the creature which survives not by adapting to the environment but by adapting the environment, has been selected with an inbuilt drive to control his own circumstances,[16] and that he aspires, despite himself, to be not merely the measure of all things but the master of all things. What counts as an "effective" grasp of the fundamental workings of a system is an understanding that will enable one to compute forthcoming events, and be able to *act* on the basis of that assumption.

The prime object of scientific activity is that man will acquire an increasing ability to predict the behavior of external objects and forces. Science makes progress whenever our ability to predict the observed universe is greater or more accurate than it was before. A "good" scientific model is thus one which increases our ability to do this, and a "bad" model is one which does not. What we seek in our models is the ability on our part to use them to better achieve the purpose of scientific activity. In architecture or in engineering we often construct physical, small-scale models to assist us to solve our problems. The function of the model is to "stand in" for the real thing which it represents, be it a building, a bridge, or an airplane. We hope that the relationship of the parts of the model to each other will enable us to say something about the relationship between the equivalent aspects of the real thing. If our model office block is built to scale in size, weight, and strength, and we see that it collapses when we add more than twenty stories to the foundations, then—if it is a good model—we would consider ourselves unwise to build a real office block with as many as twenty stories unless we first adopt a stronger design for the foundations. The model, while not describing reality, tells us something about it by way of the internal relationships between its parts.

We can, of course, construct models which tell us something from external relationships with other models. When we build our model airplane, we do so in order to see if a particular design is viable. We expose it in a wind tunnel to a model of the airstream which the real airplane will have to fly through. If our modeling has been good, it is our hope that the relationship between the model airplane and the model airstream will tell us something about the relationship between the real airplane and the real airstream.

Similarly, we hope that our scientific models will tell us something about the behavior of the observed universe. Even though scientific models are not generally physical, but models in the sense of ideas, our hope is that study and computation performed on them will tell us something of how to predict the observed universe. Consider, for example, the "model" formulation of gravitational attraction. It was worded thus: "I propose that in order to understand our observed reality, we should contemplate a mental model of it in which bodies attract each other with a force that varies inversely with the square of the distance between them." If, by manipulation with this model, by performing calculations on it, we are able to "predict" what we already know occurs in the observed universe (i.e., to "retrodict"), then obviously our model has some value. If, by similar calculation on the model, we are able to predict events in the universe whose outcome we do not already know, then we say that the model is a good one. We say it is good because the relationship between aspects of the model "stands in" for an equivalent relationship in the observed universe, and because contemplation of the model has enabled us to extend our predictive power over observed reality.

Two things are required of our models for them to serve our scientific purposes. They must "stand in" for the observed universe in two respects. The relationships *within* the model must enable us to increase our ability to predict the aspect of observable reality which the model represents, and the relationships *between* the new model and other models must reflect the equivalent relationships in the world of our observation. In other words, we ask of our scientific model system that its behavior will enable us to predict observable reality, and that it be internally consistent. A new model, such as an equation for falling bodies, might be valuable to us if it enables us to predict what will happen to objects which fall. It will be of considerably more value if it can fit consistently into a general model of motion and thereby enormously extend our predictive range.

When we test proposed models in science, then, we are testing them for their capacity for helping us achieve the ends of the activity. We test the model to see if it enables us to predict new things about the world of our observation, and whether it is consistent with our already established model system—the one we call our scientific knowledge. We constantly attempt to improve our scheme of analogues, in order that our ability to predict the observed universe may be extended. When we reject a previously used model in favor of a newly proposed one, we do so because testing shows us that the new one is more adequate to our purposes than the old. Einstein's model was preferred over Newton's because it enabled us to predict everything about the observed universe which Newton's did, *and a little extra.* It was not that Newton's theory was "falsified"—as we saw, there are logical reasons for supposing such a process to be impossible. Rather, it was that Einstein's theory served our purposes better.

Of course, there remains the problem whether to admit a new model in the event of inconsistency with our established system of analogues, or whether to propose, instead, that the established system is inadequate. Now that we are using concepts which make clear the element of human motivation in the activity, the problem seems less acute. It is not a question of rejecting possible truth, or even admitting falsehoods. It comes down to a question of the relative adequacy of the alternatives for the task we have set them. Where the new proposal has successful predictive ability, but cannot be rendered consistent with existing models (i.e., it fails to "predict" established knowledge), the need for research to decide whether the new or the established model can be modified in order to achieve consistency is clearly indicated. Sometimes both may apply. The obvious example from the history of science pertains to theories about the nature of light. Corpuscular theories were useful models in that they could explain some observed phenomena and be used to predict new events. Wave theories could be used to explain other observed phenomena, and could also predict. Consistency was only achieved after two centuries, when a model system (the quantum theory) was proposed that was to some extent a compromise, combining elements of both rival systems.

We can, if necessary, reject such proposals as Prout's atomic weight theory without feeling that we might be rashly consigning to oblivion an important truth. All we are rejecting is what might turn out to be a useful model after all. If we proceed in this fashion, and have inadvertently rejected a useful model, there will be plenty of opportunities to reconsider its merits at such time in the future as we find that other discrepancies have led to the need for a major overhaul of our established system of analogues. The point is worth making that the Prouts of science are quite rare. Usually when we discard proposed models after testing, we never regret doing so. It is better to discard the occasional good model along with the many, many bad ones (knowing we can pick it up later) than to proceed overcautiously, spending overmuch time on the consideration of worthless models.

It is important to appreciate that we are not concerned with the notion of "adequacy" in any absolute sense. Only a scheme of models whose contemplation enabled us to predict and explain everything within the world of our observation could be deemed "adequate" in that sense. What concerns us is that we should select at each stage a model which is *more* adequate than its rivals in helping us predict or retrodict. Our testing, therefore, is necessarily *competitive*. We choose the comparatively more adequate, and we seek increased predictive power—a relative factor. When we test, therefore, we are testing relatively. We are testing to discover which of the proposed alternative models best serves our purposes. At first glance, this stress on the competitive aspect of testing might appear to run counter to experience: surely there are cases in which a new model is proposed to help us understand a newly observed phenomenon? In fact, though, we always have, at the very least, a simple background theory which previously satisfied us. In the case of a "newly observed phenomenon," we can reflect on Popper's dictum that we make "observations" only in the light of our previous theories.[17] An event strikes our notice as an observation only when there is a preconceived theory; we single it out for attention because it assumes significance to us against the background of that preconceived theory.

Even Newton's theory had its predecessors in the form of models which postulated that for things to fall downward was a natural state of affairs. It was Newton's model, on which objects continued at rest or in constant velocity, which made the downward acceleration of objects require additional causes. The theory which proposes as its model that a given state of affairs is "natural" is as much a theory as a successor which proposes that additional causes must be sought. When we test, we reject whichever alternative is less adequate to our task of predicting the observed universe.

We can now think of scientific activity as a human discipline in which the participants attempt to approach ever nearer to a nominated objective. The fact that the objective (perfect knowledge) is not obtainable in the absolute sense in no way prevents us from approaching ever nearer to it than we were before. The method of science consists in the nomination of proposed models, whose function is to enable us, by studying their relationships, to make successful predictions concerning the universe which we can observe. We constantly increase our ability to predict by competitively selecting models on their ability to assist us in that task. More accurately, we reject those which are shown, on testing, to be less adequate than the alternatives. Scientific activity, then, has several important ingredients.

All of those who engage in science are expected to embrace the nominated objective of increased predictive power; and they know that their performance within the activity will be adjudged successful insofar as they are able to achieve such an increase. They might be kindly, humane men; they might be a source of inspiration to their students; they might stand out as worthy of admiration for taking moral stands on the political uses of scientific knowledge. But they will be judged as successful scientists only by the standard which requires them to increase man's ability to predict the observed universe.

Secondly, it may be said of science that its activity consists of the construction and proposition of mental models, and in the testing of these models. Scientific activity requires that men imagine analogue systems whose study will enable successful predictions to be made concerning the observed universe. It requires the exercise of the imagination in order that testing programs might be produced which are designed to bring competing model systems to a "crisis point" at which one can be selected as superior to its rivals. And it requires this process to be continuous. Science makes progress toward its nominated end whenever a decision is taken. At every crisis point a less adequate model is rejected in favor of a more adequate model; and since adequacy is measured by the ability to achieve the nominated end, it follows automatically that every decision takes us nearer to the nominated end. Even when the decision at the crisis point is to reject the newly proposed model on the grounds that it is less adequate than the established model, we know at least that the rejected model can be eliminated in our search for superior ones.

Trial and Error

Sometimes in such circumstances we gain even more assistance in our efforts. If the devisor of the test has been particularly skillful, or particularly lucky, we might get direct feedback and learn not only that a particular proposed model was less adequate but also the respects in which it was inadequate. We might learn, in other words, how to improve the model in such a way that it becomes superior to its rivals. Even without such circumstances, however, we proceed by negative feedback, continually eliminating the worse in favor of the better.

The normal course of scientific activity is thus one in which every alteration to our system of analogues is an improvement: it was only admitted after testing had shown it to be better than its predecessors. Progress is, in science, the norm. The activity proceeds in such a way that every decision must mean an advancement, either in introducing a new model which better fulfills our goal of increased predictive power or in making us aware that at least one type of model is not what we are looking for if we are to augment that power.

It might be argued that "mistakes" are possible in this scheme of scientific activity; that it is possible for us to discard a good model in favor of one which seems better at the time but subsequently turns out to be inferior. It is certainly true that circumstances like these can arise, but it would be wrong to think of the period in which the old (good) model was set aside as a blind alley or a retrogression. If a new model is preferred, it must be because a critical test or series of tests has shown it to have improved predictive power over the old model (our "crisis point"). If the old one is subsequently rehabilitated in modified form, it will be for a similar reason. Both stages, the rejection and subsequent readoption, are marked by an extension of our predictive power, and both, therefore, represent progress toward our goal. It is the period spent with the new model which shows us the inadequacies which only a modified form of the old model can surmount.

Had there been no "blind alley" phase, we have no reason to suppose that our old model would have been so improved. Provided we act in science in full consciousness of what we are doing and what we are trying to achieve, progress is guaranteed with every decision we make.

We cannot, of course, guarantee that when we perform our tests we are not in a state in which our senses are deceiving us. One of the weaknesses of "falsification" is that we can never be sure that our observations are made accurately, and that we are right to reject the theory instead of our sensory evidence. Can it not also be said of our model systems that we might reject a good one because we observe test results incorrectly? The important point of difference between the two approaches is that the "falsification" approach concerns itself with true or false propositions concerning "the facts" whereas the model system concerns itself with analogues designed to help us predict the observable universe.

It may be true that our senses might deceive us in one test; but since tests have to be repeatable, one such freak occurrence would easily be corrected. The more serious case we are considering is one in which our senses repeatedly and consistently deceive us, so that other experimenters, performing repetitions of the test, will achieve equally erroneous results. If, however, such a situation occurs, it may readily be seen that the achieved result *is* the observed universe, whether or not it diverges from some unknown and unknowable reality. If our senses consistently deceive us at some point, then our model systems will be so constructed as to predict that deception. They will not enable us to appreciate that it is a deception, but our concern is with what we observe, with predicting the *observed* universe. We can leave those whose concern is with "truth" and "the facts" to worry about whether their observations accord with what really is the case. With our more limited objective of being able to predict what we will observe, the problem does not arise at all. We reject whichever of our proposed models is less adequate than its rival at enabling us to predict the observed universe—less adequate, that is, at enabling us to predict the *observed* results of our tests, as opposed to any "real" results of our tests.

In view of the remarks made earlier concerning reality and the form in which it cannot but present itself to us, it is very doubtful that there is anything to be gained from drawing a distinction between "reality" and "reality-as-we-can-observe-it." Since any reality objective of the minds and sense organs of the species which contemplate it can only be interpreted by any individual species through its mind and sense organs, the contemplation of it can avail us naught. Our limited concern in science is to produce analogue systems whose contemplation will enable us to predict successfully what we shall observe in any tests we perform.

We are now in a position where we are able to supply a conceptual modification to Popper's shorthand formula of scientific method.[18] Popper describes the system by the terms

$$P_1 \to TT \to EE \to P_2$$

meaning that proposition 1 proceeds by way of theory testing and error elimination to proposition 2, which itself becomes the P_1 of a new cycle of the formula. Each P_2, says Popper, is necessarily more accurate than P_1 by virtue of the error eliminated as a consequence of theory testing. Thus is progress made in science.

With consideration to the criticism given above, we can keep the essential aspect of the formula, the "conjecture and refutation" side of it, but modify the concepts to give us a new formula:

$$M_1 \text{ or } M_2 \to T \to CP \to IE \to M_2$$

This is a shorthand way of saying that we proceed from the competitive proposal of model systems (M_1 and M_2) by way of testing (T) to a crisis point (CP), at which we can eliminate the less adequate of the competitors (IE, or inadequacy elimination), finally arriving at a preferred M_2. The successful

M_2 will then have competing M_3 proposed against it, and will undertake a new cycle of the formula.

M_1 represents the model which corresponds to our latest stage of knowledge. It was preferred at some point because testing showed it to be more adequate than its rivals at enabling us to predict the observed universe. M_2 is the new scientific conjecture that is proposed as a better model. Tests are designed which will bring the competing systems to a crisis point, at which we will have grounds for preferring one rather than the other. Those grounds are the superiority of one system at helping us predict what we shall observe. The less adequate of the two is eliminated, and we are left with a new "current state of knowledge," M_2, which we know will one day be superseded by a superior competitor.

The conventional aspects of this equation are explicit. We are choosing between alternatives on the basis of which one best serves our intentions. We deliberately undertake testing to bring us to a crisis point at which we can satisfy ourselves as to which best serves those intentions. We are not eliminating objective error from propositions, we are deciding which one we prefer. The testing is equivalent to a practical run under field conditions: the one which performs better under testing is chosen because it has proved itself in practice.

"Inadequacy elimination" is the stage at which we eliminate whichever model shows itself in practice to be of less assistance to us in our chosen task of successfully predicting the world of our observation. Progress is guaranteed. Each M_2 is necessarily superior for our purposes than each M_1; it was chosen only for that reason. Furthermore, this revised formula purports to describe not only what scientists *should* do but what they *do* do. We are now in a position to appreciate why science has made the "constant and linear" progress referred to in Chapter 1. Science has made progress because its participants have accepted the nominated end of the activity,

Trial and Error

and because a method has been used which guarantees that every step is a step forward.

The method by which one model is replaced by another guarantees that we retain our best devices for predicting the observed universe until we have satisfied ourselves that there are better ones. At no point do we detach ourselves from any rung of the ladder until we have one foot on another rung we know to be higher. Given a common acceptance of the direction of our destination, it is inevitable that each move should be a move toward it. We may reduce the constituent elements of progress in science to two:

1. Universal acceptance by the participants of the nominated end (ability to predict the observed universe as much as possible)
2. Adoption by the participants of the method outlined by the formula M_1 or $M_2 \rightarrow T \rightarrow CP \rightarrow IE \rightarrow M_2$

(We might note that there is a third, implied condition: that scientists will exercise their imaginations to create new, conjectured model systems [M_2s] and that they, or others, will use their imaginative skills to devise tests which can bring the competition of alternatives to a critical point at which choice can be made. But this condition amounts only to saying that there must be scientists who engage in scientific activity.)

Given those conditions, scientific progress will be made, even if it is only the progress which covers an increasing knowledge of what proposed model systems are *not* more adequate than established ones. As we might expect from simple observation of the history of science, highly talented and imaginative individuals within the discipline can make a considerable difference to the rate of progress achieved. Progress of a much more direct and appreciable kind is made when an M_2 supplants an M_1; so it is a good thing for scientific progress if great minds work on the problem of creating new models.

Again, scientific progress is obviously accelerated if talented people work on the problems concerned with devising critical tests. It would be remarkable indeed if the progress of science were smooth and regular, despite the different mental qualities of those who, at various times, have engaged in the activity. It has not been. Its rate has varied with the quality and numbers of its participants; but it has been linear and unidirectional. Every decision has represented a step nearer the perhaps unattainable goal of ability to predict everything.

We should note that the scientific conjectures of model systems represent *attempts* to achieve the chosen goal. If we were being less specific, we could, without inaccuracy, replace M_1 and M_2 by A_1 and A_2, where A_1 represents the best *attempt* thus far to reach toward the desired end and A_2 is the proposed improvement. We embark upon the course of action in order to fulfill a human purpose (in this case the ability to predict the observed universe). Each proposed model is an attempt to achieve that purpose more or better than previous attempts. We can thus restate our constituent elements of progress in science as

1. Universal acceptance by the participants of the nominated end
2. Adoption by the participants of the method outlined by the formula A_1 or $A_2 \rightarrow T \rightarrow CP \rightarrow IE \rightarrow A_2$

Once the constituent elements are put into this form, we can see that there are no longer any terms within these conditions which refer specifically and exclusively to *scientific* activity. We have replaced Popper's *propositions,* P_1 and P_2, by *attempts* to achieve the aim of the activity. (We note that in science they take the form of proposing models M_1 and M_2.) We have substituted *testing* for Popper's *theory* testing, and we have replaced the idea of *error* elimination by *inadequacy* elimination. By taking out the terms which referred to propositions, theories, and errors, we have taken the equation out of the limited realm of science, and we can see that scientific activity represents only a special case determined by condition 1, the aim of the activity. These twin constituents of scientific progress can be seen as constituents of progress which have specific application in the field of science.

What gives scientific progress its peculiarly "scientific" character are the specific terms we write, as a special case, into those two general constituent elements of progress. It is because the nominated end, universally accepted by the participants, is the ever-increasing ability to predict the world of our observation, and because the attempts to achieve this (A_1 and A_2) take the form of proposed models (M_1 and M_2), that the progress becomes, in this instance, scientific progress. It would be nonsense to ask such questions as "Suppose science had different aims?" because the aim itself is an important defining characteristic of the activity. It becomes an equal absurdity to ask questions concerning "scientific theories which cannot be tested," since such theories would fall outside the ambit of the application of condition 2, and would therefore not be scientific. If a proposal cannot be tested, we cannot proceed through the stages represented by the equation, and we cannot either prefer it over its rivals or reject it.

In one sense, even questions of the form "But *should* science proceed in this manner?" are bogus. It is sensible to suggest that scientists should adopt a particular way of doing things if they wish to achieve their objectives, but it should be appreciated that it is the pursuit of those objectives by the method described by condition 2 which defines the activity. If people nominate alternative goals, or proceed to them by other methods, then they are not engaging in scientific activity at all. The analysis given above purports to be a description of the elements of scientific progress. To suggest that people *should* do things in another way is to suggest that they engage in activities other than the pursuit of scientific progress. The analysis, in other words, claims to be an examination of what people *must* and *do* do when they undertake scientific research.

It is quite possible that many practicing scientists might be found who would deny that the above analysis accurately describes their activities. It is well to remember, in this context, that most scientists thought (and some still do) that they were using inductive processes to arrive at general theories; and that this belief continued long after the logical impossibility of induction had been illustrated. We judge scientists as good or bad on the basis of their ability to perform the activity, not to understand it or explain it. Our contention is that the two constituent elements, conditions 1 and 2, suffice to give an account of the activity and the reasons for its progress, whether or not those actually engaged in the exercise fully appreciate this.

It cannot be doubted that many scientists pursue their activities with motives other than seeking to extend our predictive power. Desire for financial gain, for Nobel prizes, for the esteem of one's peers—all play a part in motivation. They might all be determining factors which decide people to propose new models or to devise sophisticated tests. The point is that because the conventional target is the extension of predictive power, success or failure of scientists as scientists is judged by that standard. A scientist such as Lysenko, who gained wealth and power in Stalinist Russia, is not regarded as a good or successful scientist because he is not judged by his own motives, but by the conventional object of science.

For Kuhn to say, as he does, "There remains the problem of understanding why progress should be so noteworthy a characteristic of an enterprise conducted with the techniques and goals this [i.e., his] essay has described,"[19] is for him to tell us that he has failed to understand correctly the techniques and goals of science. As we have seen from the above analysis, progress is inevitable once conditions 1 and 2 are satisfied.

Kuhn's treatment of scientific revolutions seems as much a psychological as a philosophical study. No doubt there are factors which induce scientists to work from an assumed "paradigm," and doubtless, too, the young generation of scientists reacts against the authority of its elders and is more inclined to accept revolutionary paradigms. But none of this really deals with the standards by which scientists are judged, whatever their psychological motivating factors. No scientist would urge acceptance of a new paradigm on the grounds that it would enable a new generation to assert its independence from its teachers. And if one did, certainly no one would pay attention to him. This might be his basic motivation, but to gain acceptance (or at least favorable consideration), he would have to show how the new paradigm is better than the old model in its uses for prediction.

In dwelling on the importance of paradigms, Kuhn singles out for special attention what is only one aspect of scientific development. There are times, it is true, when our scheme of analogues stands in need of major structural alteration. There are periods when anomalies and discrepancies pile up from testing, and the scientific community realizes that its particular model must undergo a major overhaul if its predictive power is to be enlarged without loss to consistency. Such a situation prevailed in nuclear physics and electromagnetic radiation toward the end of the nineteenth and the beginning of the twentieth century. A whole new range of observed phenomena could not be predicted successfully by existing models, and a major search was undertaken on several fronts for replacements. But the scientific "revolution" is only a magnified version of what goes on all the time in scientific activity. How much change must there be to a model before it can be called a new "paradigm"? How new must new ways of thinking be before we can talk of "revolution"? Such questions lead us to appreciate that, in talking of scientific revolutions, we are discussing questions of scale, not kind. Every improvement of a paradigm is a change of model, whether this be "within" the paradigm or beyond it.

Kuhn's paradigms assume, for him, considerable importance in the consideration of scientific progress. "Part of the answer to the problem of progress," he says, "lies simply in the eye of the beholder." "It is only during periods of normal science that progress seems both obvious and assured."[20] He takes the phrase *normal science* to describe the situation in which there are no competing paradigms struggling for supremacy, and he uses the term *progress* to denote "the result of successful creative work." He is telling us that it is only when there is a universal paradigm that "successful creative work" (within that paradigm) will be recognized for the progress that it is. It is not recognized during times of intense paradigm competition because the "very fundamentals" are questioned. If Kuhn is telling us, in a rather elaborate way, that the improvement of models is recognized as progress except at such times as people think the whole model stands in need of major alteration in structure, then he is saying nothing controversial. But we must not lose sight of the fact that, given the nominated aim of science to extend our predictive ability, progress represents an actual increase in our capacity for successful prediction, quite regardless of whether it is recognized at the time or is overlooked because it derives from a "wrong" paradigm.[21] Given a clear aim, progress can be measured objectively by the degree to which that aim is attained.

Even though this analysis is presented as a description of what scientists must and *do* do when they engage in scientific activity, inspection of the conditions can lead to the postulation that certain prevailing conditions are more conducive to scientific progress than others. It may be taken for granted that acceptance of the nominated aim is a necessary condition for progress; otherwise there would be no target to make

Trial and Error

progress toward. What can by no means be taken for granted is that scientific progress will proceed at the same rate, regardless of conditions prevailing in society and in the scientific community. Some of the factors represented by terms in the formula

$$M_1 \text{ or } M_2 \rightarrow T \rightarrow CP \rightarrow IE \rightarrow M_2$$

can be influenced by society's institutional arrangements and traditions. We are more likely to encounter the proposition of useful models if many, rather than few, are engaged in the activity and if no arbitrary bars are placed on the type of models which may be proposed. If a society, for ideological or religious or other reasons, deliberately prohibits formulation of models within a certain range, it is denying science access to a group of possibly useful proposals, and might well find its scientific progress retarded. Similarly with the T stage of the method. We expect progress to be fastest where there are fewest limits to testing. If there is freedom to test, and resources are available for testing, then we would expect these conditions to be more conducive to progress than their opposites. And of course it follows that if a community insists on the retention of certain models, without allowing them to be replaced, then here, too, progress is denied.

These conditions are almost the opposite of those which Kuhn alleges to prevail during periods of most progress. Kuhn alleges (correctly, I think) that scientific communities behave in a restrictive manner.[22] To obtain professional recognition *at the time,* a practicing scientist is expected to conform. The scientific community tends to cold-shoulder those who do not "accept the paradigm." As often as not, they are dismissed as cranks and excluded from the respect of their peers. Despite apparent freedom to conjecture, to test, and to replace models, the pressure of the community often makes the exercise of this freedom very difficult for the scientist who wishes to remain in good standing with the scientific profession. These are the characteristics of those periods in which Kuhn says the paradigm is unchallenged: the periods of "normal" science. And yet, says Kuhn, these are the very periods in which there is unchallenged progress.

On the basis of our examination of the conditions required for progress, and how the individual factors might be optimized, we can only look upon the restrictive tendencies of scientific communities as unfortunate limitations on possible progress. The practices of the professional body of scientists during periods of "normal" science can only restrict the range and scope of proposed models and tests, and inhibit, rather than accelerate, the rate of progress. If scientific workers did not have to fear disapproval and rejection by their peer group, they might be much freer in their creative thought and work, and might accelerate progress in consequence. The oft-declared ideals of the scientific community—objectivity, fair-mindedness, willingness to consider any point—are much more appropriate to the conditions required for progress than its narrow-minded practices.

Looked at more objectively, without the confusion of considering what people think at the time, we can see that the scientific "revolutions" are regarded as much more the periods of greatest progress than are the quieter, "normal" times. When there is a major restructuring of our model system, such that a new group of phenomena is successfully brought within range of our predictive power, we speak of dramatic progress being made. This is what we would expect from our analysis, for it is at such times that the exposed weaknesses of the established model system lessen the pressure for conformity which the scientific community is able to bring to bear. It is at such times that the attention of many minds is directed to the problem, and that people are working on a wide variety of alternatives and test situations.

Popper has introduced the idea of a "Third World" (or "World III") in which our propositions, once uttered, gain objectivity.[23] Unlike World I (the world of external fact) or

Trial and Error

World II (the world of ourselves, our thoughts and our emotions), World III is concerned with those ideas which we put forward as conjectures. One of the important points he makes about World III is that the propositions we put into it become detached from ourselves and from our lives. They become "objectified," in that they stand to be criticized only on their merits, and independently of the life and motive of the persons who formulated them. Without necessarily accepting Popper's "tripartite" division, or even his categories, it is useful to think in terms of his World III when we think about scientific progress. Kuhn thinks of progress as something totally subjective, and so it is in at least one sense. Obviously, any individual's idea of what steps constitute progress will be determined by the aims he envisages. As was said in Chapter 1, one man's progress is another man's retrogression.

There is, however, a sense in which progress can be thought of more objectively. The public delineation of an activity by a nominated aim *does* objectify that activity, and provides a standard by which performance in that activity can be judged, without regard to the individual aims of those who participate. It is as if science as a discipline has had its objectives placed into a kind of World III. The aim of science, to increase ability to predict the observed universe, has been objectified beyond the reach of the professional body of scientists. While they might bestow praise on conformist behavior, and blame on the independent mavericks of the discipline, they are no longer in any position to control the judgment over what behavior is "scientific" or what proposed models constitute "progress." Such things are now judged against the measuring rod which lies beyond their reach, in World III.[24]

In talking of the progress which, to Kuhn, seems so conspicuously absent in nonscientific fields, he says: "If we doubt, as many do, that non-scientific fields make progress, that cannot be because individual schools make none. Rather it must be because there are always competing schools, each of which constantly questions the very foundations of the others."[25] His claim is that while there is progress in each school, by "successful creative work," there is no progress in the field as a whole because each school attacks the legitimacy of every other school. If we consider a single school within the field, for the moment, we can ask, pertinently, how "successful" creative work is to be distinguished from "unsuccessful" creative work. By what standard is success measured? If there is progress within an individual school, it can only be in the form of a nearer approach to whatever that school regards as the end of its activity. And if other schools do not admit that this change can be described as progress, even though it be a nearer approach to the aim of the school which produced it, it must be because they are not in agreement with that school on the objectives of the activity. These "very fundamentals" that are called into question are, in fact, views about the end sought by the exercise.

If these nonscientific fields were agreed, within each discipline, upon the objective sought, they could hope to establish by testing whether any new proposal from one particular school represented a nearer approach to that end. Acceptance by the various schools that compose a discipline of an agreed-upon paradigm is largely irrelevant. Even without a paradigm, they can test to see which of the proposed paradigms best enables the objective to be achieved. Whereas if they have a paradigm but no clear sight of their objective, then testing is rendered meaningless since they have nothing to test for. What is missing from these activities in which no progress is made is not agreement on a paradigm but agreement on an objective.

We say that the two conditions for progress, 1 and 2, contained no terms relating exclusively to scientific activity. What they jointly describe is a process by which attempts to achieve a chosen end converge on the ever-increasing fulfillment of that end. But both conditions must be met before progress can be made. When Kuhn talks about the questioning of "very fundamentals" by opposing schools as the reason for lack of overall progress within any particular field, we can point out, more accurately, that condition 1 is not being fulfilled. Those who disagree about what is to be done can never agree about the value of what has been done. But those who *do* agree about what is to be done can find in the formula of our condition 2 a method which will enable them to converge on its achievement. Science is one activity in which progress has been made through using a convergent method to achieve an agreed-upon objective. As I intend to show, there are others.

Notes

[1] The chief exposition of Popper's account of scientific method is to be found in *The Logic of Scientific Discovery* (1959).

[2] Sir Karl Popper, *Objective Knowledge* (1972), ch. 2, "Two Faces of Common Sense," p. 42.

[3] Ibid.

[4] Ibid.

[5] Ibid.

[6] Ibid., sec. 23.

[7] From ch. 1 of Popper's *Conjectures and Refutations*. Popper discusses the asymmetry between verifiability and falsifiability in his *Logic of Scientific Discovery,* ch. 1, sec. 6, and more fully in sec. 22 of his "Postscript."

[8] Imre Lakatos, *Criticism and the Growth of Knowledge* (1970), edited with Alan Musgrave. Paper by Lakatos, "Falsification and the Methodology of Scientific Research Programmes."

[9] Ibid.

[10] Popper himself rejects the role of "belief" in scientific inquiry. In his *Objective Knowledge* (ch. 2) he points out that "if much depends upon our belief, then *not only the intensity* of the belief changes, but its whole biological function" (his italics). In his example, he illustrates that an outcome which puts the life of a best friend at stake can make even the most trivial proposition require reassurance.

[11] *Logic of Scientific Discovery,* sec. 19, contains Popper's critique of conventionalism.

[12] Lakatos says, in his essay "Falsification and the Methodology of Scientific Research Programmes": "But even this appeal procedure cannot do more than *postpone* the conventional decision. For the verdict of the appeal court is not infallible either. When we decide whether it is the replacement of the 'interpretative' or of the 'explanatory' theory that produces novel facts, we again must take a decision about the acceptance or rejection of basic statements."

[13] From the essay in *Criticism and the Growth of Knowledge,* p. 138.

[14] Thomas S. Kuhn, *The Structure of Scientific Revolutions,* vol. 2, no. 2, of International Encyclopedia of Unified Science.

[15] This, at least, is the conventionally nominated aim of the activity. How the real aims of men are linked to that nominated end is discussed later.

[16] I am suggesting here that it might be helpful to think of man's activities as governed ultimately by a subset of the general evolutionary laws. Just as Newton supplied a unifying formula for laws of motion by presenting

(1) Unification : Gravitational force
(2) Modus operandi : Inverse square law

so did Darwin unify biological development by presenting the two-part formula

(1) Unification : Survivability
(2) Modus operandi : Mutation and selection

(Although it was the post-Darwinians who refined it into this form.)

I am suggesting that man's social activities are ultimately governed by this two-part formula and that they may be unified with a subset of it in which we have

(1) Unification : Control over circumstance
(2) Modus operandi : Trial and inadequacy elimination

The suggestion is that man engages in activities with a view (whether consciously held or not) to placing himself above the vicissitudes of fortune, to rendering himself invulnerable to the random hazards of the universe, and that he proceeds in this direction by testing competing attempts and eliminating the ones which serve his purposes less adequately than others.

[17] Popper contrasts the "bucket" theory of the mind, in which we are supposed to move through life with observations being scooped up as they cross our path, with the "searchlight" theory, in which we *notice* that which strikes our attention as significant in some way. He points out the problem with the former theory, which lies in "selecting" what to observe. About any one situation there is an infinite number of observations which can be made. The ones we pick upon are those which assume significance in the light of a preconceived theory.

[18] Given in Popper's *Objective Knowledge,* in the third essay: "Epistemology without a Knowing Subject" (1972).

[19] Thomas S. Kuhn, *The Structure of Scientific Revolutions* (1962), ch. XIII: "Progress through Revolutions."

[20] Ibid.

[21] Kuhn draws no clear distinction between what *is* progress and what is *recognized* as progress. He says, for instance: "Revolutions close with a total victory for one of the two opposing camps. Will that group ever say that the result of its victory has been something less than progress? That would be rather like admitting that they had been wrong and their opponents right. To them, at least, the outcome of revolution must be progress, and they are in an excellent position to make certain that future members of their community will see past history in the same way."

And later: "Inevitably those remarks will suggest that the member of a mature scientific community is, like the typical character of Orwell's *1984,* the victim of a history rewritten by the powers that be. Furthermore, that suggestion is not altogether inappropriate."

[22] Ibid.

[23] Introduced in his 1972 lecture to the Mont Pelerin Society and dealt with in his *Objective Knowledge* (1972).

[24] Although Kuhn says in his *Structure of Scientific Revolutions* that the professional community is the custodian of the aims and rules of science. He says: "The group's members, as individuals and by virtue of their shared training and experience, must be seen as the sole possessors of the rules of the game or of some equivalent basis for unequivocal judgements."

The view I express above runs directly counter to Kuhn. Science,

as a recognized activity, is beyond the reach of any particular generation of practitioners.
[25]Ibid.

3
A New Demarcation

A proposition which purports to concern itself with reality and yet has no implied consequences detectable in the observed universe is at once a source of puzzlement and irritation to thinkers of empirical bent. Empiricists (and others) have rightly felt that there is an important difference in kind between scientific conjectures, which have added so much to our interpretation of and our ability to predict the observed universe, and those more speculative fancies which do not appear to concern themselves with any reality that man can hope to get to grips with. Conjectures which have no implications for the world of our observation cannot be subjected to the formula described in our condition 2. They cannot be tested, nor can competitors be brought to a crisis point at which there can be a decision to eliminate the less adequate. Because they represent bewildering anomalies in an otherwise smoothly running system, philosophers of some schools have sought to eliminate them from consideration; and it is this desire to dismiss these "metaphysical" propositions which lies at the heart of the "demarcation debate."

The attempt of the Vienna Circle of logical positivists[1] was to establish standards of meaningfulness which metaphysical propositions would fail. Whereas the established common-sense view of meaning would have it that two conditions must be satisfied before a proposition can be considered meaningful, namely:

1. The language in the propositional statement must be used correctly, and
2. The words contained in the proposition must themselves be meaningful,

the Vienna Circle maintained that a third condition must also be satisfied:

3. The words must express either a tautology or a proposition which is capable, at least in principle, of being verified.

It may be seen that while metaphysical propositions might hope to pass 1 and 2, they would undoubtedly fail 3, and could therefore be dismissed as "literal nonsense."

This approach has the advantage for empiricists that they need take no notice of metaphysical propositions. If these lie beyond the demarcation line, they are meaningless and can be ignored. The disadvantage is that the procedure is unsound. Not only does the notion of "verification" demand impossible proof that our senses do not deceive us when we attempt to verify anything, it rules out many of the most important conjectures of the natural sciences. A general law of nature can never be verified, since it purports to account for every specific instance of a general rule. We can never observe every possible case and cannot, therefore, verify the law.[2] Thus if verification is a standard of meaningfulness, all our physical "laws of nature" are nonsense.

Some philosophers (but notably not Popper) have tried to remedy the defect by substituting the notion of "falsification" for verification in the extra requirement for meaningfulness.[3] Again, not only is there the same problem of a reliance on sensory evidence, but a whole class of innocent-sounding propositions of the form "Perpetual motion machines exist" would be reduced to gibberish. Obviously, such propositions could never be falsified, since one would need to inspect simultaneously all parts of the universe to establish that there is none (even if one could, mysteriously, assume that one is observing reliably).

The failure of any of these proposed additional requirements for meaningfulness to gain wide acceptance derives, in part, from the fact that they all involve us in throwing away too many important babies with the metaphysical bathwater. The failure derives, too, from the lack of any objectivity in the establishment of such requirements. Even if all the parties opposed to metaphysics were to agree on a third requirement, and even if it were one that enabled the conjectures of the natural sciences to be retained, the way would still be open for those who indulge in metaphysical speculation to simply record their disagreement.[4] They might claim, with justice, that no objective standard required them to accept any requirement for meaningfulness beyond the established commonsense requirements, 1 and 2; that the extra condition was only included to cut out metaphysics; and that since they saw no reason to exclude it, they would continue to talk what others regarded as nonsense.

The failure of the logical positivists and others to exclude metaphysics as meaningless does not mean, however, that we have to admit that there is no difference in kind between propositions which have observable implications and those which are completely speculative. Popper has looked for differences in fields other than meaningfulness. His contention is the more limited one, that metaphysical propositions do not belong in the world of science. Conceding that they may be meaningful, he relegates them to the category of non*science,* rather than non*sense.*[5] Popper's account of science may be summarized simply, but not unfairly, by saying that he regards science as an attempt to gain increasing verisimilitude ("correspondence with the facts") by trial-and-error elimination of our propositions. His shorthand formula to express this is

$$P_1 \rightarrow TT \rightarrow EE \rightarrow P_2$$

What Popper says of metaphysical propositions is that, since they are untestable, they cannot be subjected to the methods of science and must therefore be regarded as lying outside the scope of that activity. He does not deal with whether or not metaphysics can represent an attempt to obtain increasing correspondence with the facts by any method other than that of trial-and-error elimination.

What Popper has done is substantiate his claim by definition. After a rigorous analysis of what is constituted by scientific activity, he produced a tight definition of it which will not admit metaphysical activity. One cannot but admit that *if* Popper's account of science is correct, then he is certainly right to point out that metaphysics has no place in this. If science is a search for increasing truth content and lower falsity content, and if testing can enable us to eliminate error from propositions, then, obviously, an untestable proposition can never compete in the error-elimination stakes and can have no place in the activity.[6]

Although this book offers a view of science which differs in key fundamentals from Popper's accounts, it is certainly similar in this respect. The picture of science presented herein—namely, a quest for ever-increasing ability to predict the observed universe by the systematic competitive testing of alternative models and elimination, after critical testing, of those found less adequate to our purposes than their rivals—enables us to treat metaphysics in the same way. Metaphysical conjectures can be excluded from scientific activity on two grounds. Firstly, they are not designed to assist us in the task of predicting the world of observation; and secondly, since they are untestable, we can never make a choice between conflicting conjectures on the basis of which best serves our purpose.

Despite the agreement with Popper that metaphysics has no part to play in scientific activity, the implication of my findings is that Popper's exclusion of metaphysics is unnecessarily narrow and that metaphysics can be excluded from other activities as well as from science. The desire to dismiss metaphysical propositions was stated (in the first paragraph of this chapter) to lie at the heart of the demarcation debate. To my mind, this provides the key to the debate: it is a *desire* to dismiss them. The attempts of various schools to set up objective standards which will exclude metaphysics were prompted by that desire. Whether one talks of sense versus nonsense, of science versus nonscience, or of "progressive problemshift" versus "degenerating problemshift,"[7] the attempt is the same. It is to prevent us from being bothered by metaphysical theories on which we can never have any reasons for making conventional decisions. All of the proposed demarcation lines are drawn in such a way that metaphysics will lie beyond them; and they are so drawn because people do not want to have to deal with metaphysical theories.

All of these proposed standards have the weakness that they attempt to achieve one purpose by the imposition of another standard. It is a human foible, which we often encounter in daily life: we have all seen or read about countries where racial minorities are barred from voting, not because they are of the "wrong" ethnic origins but because they fail the "literacy test" or the "property test." It seems to be a human weakness that where we think our desires are somewhat disreputable, we cloak them in the garb of another standard. In the demarcation debate, it would seem that the desire to exclude metaphysics has inspired the variously proposed standards of admission. "Nonsense," "nonscience," "degenerating problemshift," and the like are all devices designed to serve a purpose substantially different from the apparent purpose. The weakness of metaphysical propositions lies in the fact that we have no way of comparing their value either with each other or with our testable propositions. I see nothing to be gained by sheltering behind an alleged objective standard—instead of admitting that this is the reason why we are determined to exclude metaphysics from our consideration. I therefore propose that we clarify the demarcation issue by stating it in the terms which best make clear our intentions; that we express our determination to take into consideration only such propositions as will allow us to take conventional decisions.

The "conventional decisions" which we take are whether to retain a proposal as more adequate or to reject it as less adequate than its rivals. And by "adequate" we refer to our ability to use it to achieve the aim of the activity. Following the criticism and modification of Popper's account of scientific method, we found ourselves left with a combination of conditions that contained no terms exclusive to science. The conditions were

1. Universal acceptance by the participants of the nominated end
2. Adoption by the participants of the method outlined by the formula A_1 or $A_2 \rightarrow T \rightarrow CP \rightarrow IE \rightarrow A_2$

In order to dispose of the insuperable objections to Popper's account, we had to produce a description of scientific progress in which the conventional aspects are much more explicit. In doing so we have arrived at conditions which will, when met, give rise to progress in activities other than science. If we agree about what is to be done, then we can compare our attempts to achieve it and select those attempts which testing reveals to be more adequate than their rivals in that respect.

What we can say about metaphysical propositions is not only that they have no place in the world of science (though we agree with Popper that this is so), but also that *we can never hope to make any progress* with regard to the alleged information content of such propositions. It may be that they are testable for factors other than their information content (this will be considered below). For the moment, however, we can say that since these propositions are, by their nature, untestable for their content, we cannot use the method outlined by the formula of condition 2 and cannot, therefore, hope to progress toward any end that might be nominated as our condition 1. Propositions which are untestable are to be rejected by an avowedly conventional decision, not because they are meaningless (which they may or may not be), or even because they are nonscientific (which they certainly are), but because they are *valueless*. We can never use them, if they are untestable, to make progress toward any end, and *therefore* we dismiss them. This *is* the reason: it needs no surreptitious support by reference to different external standards.

The nomination of an objective to gain increasing ability to predict and to retrodict the universe as we observe it, with the substitution of the more specific "proposed models" M_1 and M_2, in place of the more general "attempts," A_1 and A_2, is what makes our two-part analysis apply specifically to *scientific* activity. But untestable propositions, by lying outside the ambit of the formula of condition 2 even in its general form, can never assist us in progressing toward the achievement of any aim whatsoever. That is why they constitute "a source of puzzlement and irritation." We do not know what to do with them because *nothing* can be done with them. If metaphysical propositions were untestable in all fields, we would be unable to make conventional decisions about them in all fields.

It might seem outrageous to some that one should advocate dismissal from consideration of propositions which "might be true." The point is that whether or not they might be true has nothing whatsoever to do with our consideration of them. In principle, any proposition except a self-contradicting one "might be true." We can never have any reason for an assertion that any proposition (except a tautological or self-contradicting one) is either definitely true or definitely false. The tenor of this book is that we are not even concerned directly with truth or falsehood. But even if we were, we would still have no grounds for such an assertion. Our consideration of them is limited to their capacity to serve our ends. We do not accept a proposition as true; we retain it for the time being as more adequate than its rivals in assisting us to achieve our objectives. Similarly, we do not declare a proposition to be false; we reject it as less adequate than its rivals. Any proposition "might be true." The ones we are interested in are the ones which can, by testing, give us reason to prefer them over their rivals, or to reject them in favor of those rivals. To say that metaphysical propositions should be considered because they are meaningful and because they might be true is to say no more than that all meaningful propositions should be considered which do not actually contradict themselves.[8]

If we were to admit into our consideration the range of untestable propositions, in what form would this "consideration" manifest itself? What would we do with them? How would we evaluate them? Quite clearly, since they are untestable, we cannot be expected to compare them in respect of their ability to outperform their rivals in testing, and thus enable us to approach nearer to any objectives. We are left with them floating in the air, unanchored to the world of observation and experience, and without justification of any kind for ranking them above or below their rivals. If the proponents of untestable propositions wish to have their theories admitted to consideration, they should indicate what it is that we are supposed to do when we "consider" them. Perhaps we are expected to *believe* in them, to award them for some reason an act of faith.[9] Perhaps, by believing, we are enabled to achieve aims in life which are thought worthwhile. If this is so, then presumably the achievement can be tested, even if the content of the belief cannot.

Our new demarcation line, then, is drawn at the point of usefulness. Only testable theories can serve our aims, since only by testing can we be led to prefer some of these theories over others in respect of their ability to enable us to approach closer to the fulfillment of those aims. We can say that a proposition is useful insofar as it is testable.

There is a kind of proposition to be considered which falls in neither of the two camps. That is a proposition which, although not testable when proposed, might become testable at some subsequent date. Plainly, to those who encounter it, it falls neither in the class of testable propositions nor in the class of propositions which can never be tested. And since one cannot know in advance what advances will be made in science and technology (or other appropriate fields), there will always be some theories which, although untestable, nonetheless admit the possibility of testing at some unspecified time in the future. On which side of our new line of demarcation are we to place such propositions? If we consider, by way of example, the atomic theory of Democritus, we can appreciate that when it was formulated not only was it untestable, but no one could see any way in which it might eventually be tested.[10]

On such an issue one finds it very difficult to avoid being influenced by the knowledge that the proposal of Democritus subsequently turned out to be a model which had use in increasing our predictive power. One wishes, naturally, to adopt a procedure which would not have dismissed it. Despite this wish, there are some things which must be said about the theory. Firstly, like so many theories of the Greeks, it was completely speculative: it purported to give an account of the observable world, but in terms which, so far as Democritus and his time were concerned, not only could not be tested against competing theories but for which no one could even conceive a possible test. Secondly, the theory was at par with other, equally speculative (and contradictory) theories; and in the absence of testing, no one could have any reason for preferring some and rejecting others.

It is true that the atomic theory of Democritus (or a revised version of it) subsequently became useful; but it became useful only when it became testable. Many hundreds of years after the first formulation of the theory, when sufficient progress had been made without the use of the theory or its comparison with others for ability to predict the observed universe—only then could people have any reason to retain or reject it and to construct further models on its foundations. But at the time of its formulation, its only value lay in its potential for testability—a potential also possessed in principle by some of the countertheories of the time.

We can see from the foregoing discussion that propositions of this third type in no way present objections to a demarcation based on value. If testability is the key to value, propositions become of value to us as they become testable. Theories like that of Democritus are useful only insofar as they might become testable, in that contemplation of the theories might inspire skillful minds to work on the advances which will be required before they *do* become testable. If, as was actually the case with the theory of Democritus, there is not any conceivable way in which they might become testable, they must be set aside as nonuseful until such time as circumstances may change to admit them. But let it be remembered that propositions which are not susceptible to test and which, by their very nature, will always be untestable, will always be nonuseful.

None of this argument is calculated to establish that a proposition which is of no value in one field of endeavor might not have its uses in another. It might be claimed by those with a liking for metaphysical propositions that, even though these do not belong in the world of science, they might have their uses in other fields. It is not a claim easily established. As we saw from consideration of the general case, if attempts cannot be rated against each other by testing, we cannot hope to eliminate those that are less adequate at achieving the desired end. In other words, whenever we have an aim in view, an attempt to achieve that aim cannot assist progress unless it can be rated against other attempts by testing. Thus any untestable proposition cannot be of use to us for *any* human aim.

There are, however, propositions which are untestable in some fields but not in others. The "field" is delineated by the aim. Metaphysical propositions are those which cannot be tested for their information content. We call a proposition of the form "The Absolute is outside time" metaphysical because there is no conceivable testing program that would enable us to say whether that proposition were preferable to, say, "The Absolute is inside time." But it is quite conceivable that we might wish to use that proposition for an aim that is not concerned with its information content. Thus, while we cannot test to determine whether the proposition "The Absolute is outside time" is preferable to its rivals in increasing our ability to predict the observed universe, we can test it for a variety of other aims not directly concerned with its intelligible content. We can test, for example, to see whether the utterance of it three times at the top of a high mountain will bring rain more readily than rival utterances such as "Abracadabra"; or we can test to see if the holding of particular untestable beliefs brings about desirable rewards measured in terms of the quality of life. The belief remains untestable; but the effects consequent upon the belief *are* testable, either by the individual concerned or by others. Thus even metaphysical propositions, although untestable in the field of science or epistemology, might well be testable for their ability to assist us to achieve other aims. They might be useful where we seek either an "inspirational" effect or an effect which is "incantatory and anti-rational. A magical rather than a philosophical use of language."[11]

Lest this seem fanciful, we should reflect that a substantial body of metaphysical propositions is claimed by its adherents to have something approaching this kind of effect. While metaphysical propositions might not be useful in predicting the observed universe, it is claimed that they are useful in other ways. Propositions of a religious nature, it is claimed, enable people to lead better, more moral lives, to experience a warm glow of internal security. While they are not concerned with the pursuit of knowledge, we could hardly deny that such propositions undoubtedly have the right to be called "useful" if they can achieve such effects. The point is, though, that they are *testable* for these effects. We only call propositions "nonuseful" for fields in which they are untestable.

It may well be that the utterance of a proposition that is not testable with respect to its information content nonetheless enables other ends to be achieved. Where this is the case, it is because it is testable for those ends. An individual is in a position to test if the utterance or contemplation of a metaphysical proposition achieves "a warm glow of internal security" better than other propositions. He can even test, by his own standards, whether metaphysical propositions enable others to lead what he regards as better, more moral lives. It is because he can test these things that the metaphysical proposition becomes useful to him. He has standards by which it can be compared with its rivals. He can, in other words, proceed by the method of testing competitors and rejecting, after critical trial, those which he finds less adequate to his purposes. What those purposes are, be they internal security or a better, more moral life, is what defines the activity in which the proposition must be testable in order to be useful.

It is not correct, therefore, to say that an untestable proposition might have other uses. It is correct, however, to maintain that a proposition which is untestable in one field of activity might have its uses by being testable in another. Metaphysical propositions, we now see, can be useful, even if this usefulness is confined to objectives which can take no account of their information content (since this is, by definition, untestable). Doubtless, then, metaphysical propositions will continue to be popular. Adoption of the formal method described by the formula of condition 2 is undertaken in order to approach the objective. But people are subject to all kinds of emotions and irrational desires, and may often be, without realizing it, serving those desires rather than their declared ones. People accept what they wish to be true and whatever serves to reinforce their confirmed prejudices, even though they convince themselves that they are engaging dispassionately in extending their ability to predict the observed universe.

We should not be too surprised when people select an obviously inferior alternative, after testing, in one aspect of progress. They are, sometimes without knowing it, selecting what is a superior alternative for an aim which they esteem higher than the declared aim. Nowhere is this trait more evident than in the work of many "social scientists." They might declare their aim to be an increasing ability to predict the behavior of man and his societies, and might even think that this is what they are doing. But when it comes to the selection between competing alternatives, we often see a choice made on grounds which clearly have more to do with political and moral motives than with the desire to predict. If the tests go against a particular theory whose support lends them moral and political comfort, we often see them attack the validity of the test, rather than make a conventionally required decision which would run counter to the fulfillment of that comfort.

Retention of a clear appreciation of what constitutes the objective is a fundamental requirement for progress toward that objective. The logic of the argument herein has been that metaphysical propositions are not useful to us in that class of activity to which they purport to belong, but are often of use in the achievement of totally different (and often concealed) objectives. And it is in the pursuit of those other objectives that metaphysical propositions are testable.

One final point should be made before we move on from the demarcation issue. That is that testable attempts at achieving our aims can contribute more to the satisfaction of those aims than is gained from the simple acceptance or rejection following competitive trial. They can often assist us in the formulation of new attempts or new tests. This is what Popper calls the "fertility" of a proposition.[12] It can be called fertile, he says, if it has implications which yield a variety of wide-ranging tests and conjectures. To a great extent, this "fertility" of Popper's represents the effect that a theory has on us. If it suggests to us new avenues of approach, or sophisticated tests involving novel phenomena, then it helps us to achieve our ends by more than was originally proposed. The current jargon would probably have this as the "fallout" of the theory, that is, the unanticipated bonus of its formulation and test. We do not know very much about the mental creative process, but we can observe that inspired flashes often come about in circumstances in which proposals are subjected to criticism. Contemplation of the inadequacies of a proposal seems to assist the process of inspiration of further suggestions. We can see, therefore, since our awareness of inadequacies comes from testing, that testing can play a role in positive feedback even to the creative process itself.

This represents another point of difference between the testable and the untestable theory. Whereas the testable proposition might, under testing, make us aware of a variety of phenomena hitherto unobserved and unsuspected, and might even, by its contemplation, inspire people to devise new proposals which lack its inadequacies, the untestable proposition must, by contrast, remain completely sterile. Since it cannot be tested, it cannot open up new phenomena. It cannot enable us to ascertain its inadequacies and perhaps propose better alternatives. Unlike the testable propositions, which can open up new avenues, the metaphysical proposition remains closed. Indeed, such propositions show a disturbing tendency to reduce new discoveries into special cases of the old, rather than use new discoveries to formulate wider conjectures in which the old can be seen as a special and limited case. There are many adherents of famous metaphysical propositions who eagerly snatch up new information, revealed by testable propositions, and adduce it as yet more evidence of the universality of their theory.[13]

Having castigated untestable propositions for their lack of basis for taking conventional preference decisions, we now must add sterility to the charges against them. Not only can we not use them to progress toward our chosen ends, they do not even inspire us toward greater progress in pursuit of those ends. We can do nothing with them; and they, in turn, can do nothing for us.

There seem to be two related reasons for valuing testable rather than untestable propositions. Firstly, the testable variety provides, through tests, the basis of a conventional decision to prefer them over their rivals, or to reject them in favor of those rivals; and secondly, they can lead on to new ideas and conjectures. Neither of these reasons is concerned with the truth of a proposition, or even with whether it is retained or rejected. A proposition which has to be rejected is useful in that it tells us of yet another avenue in which we need not look for progress and of new questions which it opens up, new phenomena its testing reveals, and new conjectures which are inspired by its contemplation. Looking back over the history of scientific progress (to name only one field), we can see that many of our abandoned proposals have been of considerably more use than some of our retained ones, by virtue of the progress they have instigated even while being rejected.

Thus the decision to establish the demarcation line

openly, at the point of usefulness, is to take no account of the subsequent or possible fate of a proposition. Its usefulness is not connected with its acceptance or rejection, but rather with the fact that one or the other will take place. And it may have additional uses during the time in which we determine which of those two alternatives it shall be. For any human activity delineated by an aim, we can draw a line separating those proposals which can be tested for their ability to assist us in that activity and those which cannot. In every case we can say that only the former group will be of service to us in making progress toward the aim to which the activity is directed. The demarcation line which matters to us is the progress line: proposals which fall within it can help us progress; those which lie beyond it cannot. It is tantamount to a tautology to say that people desire to make progress toward achievement of their objectives; this is included in the idea of an objective. It is this desire, though, which has motivated the demarcation debate, a debate which has been concluded when one has injected an overt conventionalism into it. We do not want untestable propositions because they cannot help us achieve any of our aims.

Notes

[1] E.g., Rudolf Carnap, *Aufbau*. Popper points out in a footnote in his *Conjectures and Refutations* (p. 258) that although Carnap and the Vienna Circle attributed to Wittgenstein the assertion that metaphysics was meaningless and consisted of nonsensical pseudopropositions, the theory goes back to Hobbes (in one form, at least) and was used by Berkeley and Hume.

[2] Bede Rundle, in "Reforming Our Philosophical Positions" (*Encounter*, Nov. 1973), advances the view that the word *verification* has been used too rigorously. He says: "With respect to our generalisations: these are constantly being verified by the finding of particular satisfying instances." His line of argument seems to be

Trial and Error

that since we do verify, and since rigorous verification can never be possible (as Popper showed), then we must "verify" in some looser sense. I shall continue to use the word in the rigorous sense in which it is defined.

³Because Popper has been so often misquoted and misunderstood on this point, it is pertinent to point out that he has only used "falsifiability" to demarcate between "science and non-science," never between "sense and nonsense."

⁴If the meaninglessness of metaphysical propositions is purely conventional, there can always be a simple refusal to subscribe to the convention.

⁵"The criterion of meaning," says Popper, "leads to the wrong demarcation of Science and Metaphysics" (*Conjectures and Refutations,* essay 11, "The Demarcation between Science and Metaphysics").

⁶Unless increased truth content and lowered falsity content could be established by some other way than testing. I am assuming that they cannot be established except by testing in some form.

⁷The term used by Imre Lakatos in his *Criticism and the Growth of Knowledge* (edited with Alan Musgrave, 1970). Lakatos essay: "Falsification and the Methodology of Scientific Research Programmes."

⁸To explain any one event, an infinite number of meaningful explanations could be proposed, any of which "might be true." Only the testable ones provide a basis for selection between some of these competing proposals.

⁹But see ch. 2, n. 10, on the weaknesses of "belief."

¹⁰The Greeks placed no great premium on testing. Some of their scientific theories were susceptible to retrodiction; that is, they were required to account for the current state of observation. But the notion of testing by predicted consequences was never established.

¹¹The quotation is from Alasdair MacIntyre's *Marcuse* (1970). He is describing Marcuse's prose.

¹²In *Conjectures and Refutations* (1963).

¹³Also in *Conjectures and Refutations,* Popper quotes (in ch. 1) an illuminating personal experience. At a time when Adler's views on "individual psychology" were very much in vogue, Popper tells us: "Once, in 1919, I reported to him a case which to me did not

seem particularly Adlerian, but which he found no difficulty in analysing in terms of his theory of inferiority feelings, although he had not even seen the child. Slightly shocked, I asked him how he could be so sure. 'Because of my thousandfold experience,' he replied; whereupon I could not help saying: 'And with this new case, I suppose, your experience has become thousand-and-one-fold.' "

All Adler had shown was that a case could be interpreted in the light of the theory. One is reminded irresistibly of how each new historical circumstance is adduced as further "evidence" of the soundness of Karl Marx's theories on the inevitable course of historical development.

4
The Acquisition & Improvement of Skills

The notion that there might be other uses for metaphysical propositions, other than those which derive from their information content, leads to the consideration of attempts to achieve aims in which the attempts take the form of *actions*. This class of activity is clearly distinct from that which we have already inspected, in the sense that Ryle's "knowledge how" is distinct from his "knowledge that." Despite the fact that the foregoing analysis has suggested that all human activities can be delineated by a desired objective, there is still a difference which can be identified between attempts to achieve aims which proceed by way of proposition and those which involve an actual performance.

In his essay "Rationalism in Politics," Michael Oakeshott[1] sets out the two sorts of knowledge appropriate to the different types of attempts. He says:

> Every science, every art, every practical activity requiring skill of any sort, indeed every human activity whatsoever, involves knowledge. And, universally, this knowledge is of two sorts, both of which are always involved in any actual activity. It is not, I think, making too much of it to call them two sorts of knowledge, because (though in fact

they do not exist separately) there are certain important differences between them.

He calls them *technical* and *practical* knowledge.

The first of these is in many activities formulated into rules; but he tells us: "Whether or not it is, or has been, precisely formulated, its chief characteristic is that it is susceptible of precise formulation, although special skill and insight may be required to give it that formulation." The second sort he calls practical, "because it exists only in use, is not reflective and (unlike technique) cannot be formulated into rules."[2] The method by which it is shared, he claims, is "not the method of formulated doctrine." It can "neither be taught nor learned, but only imparted and acquired. It exists only in practice, and the only way to acquire it is by apprenticeship to a master—not because the master can teach it (he cannot), but because it can be acquired only by continuous contact with one who is perpetually practising it."[3]

Oakeshott's contention is that in such activities as cookery, the instructions written in a cookery book constitute only the technical knowledge. No one supposes that a person will become a good cook simply by reading the book, because there is, in addition, the practical knowledge, which can only be imparted or acquired in use.[4] His criticism of "the rationalist" stems from what Oakeshott regards as the former's assertion that this "practical knowledge" is not knowledge at all, that "properly speaking, there is no knowledge which is not technical knowledge."[5] Oakeshott does not say whether the practical knowledge can never be formulated because it is necessarily of too complex an order, or because it is nonrational, but he does, by his use of the terms *imparted* and *acquired,* make it clear that it is knowledge which can be passed from a person who knows it to one who does not, albeit by a kind of diffusion process which somehow surmounts the fact that the knowledge cannot be formulated.

Trial and Error

Oakeshott plainly takes the view that it is not merely our lack of competence at analysis or description which renders us unable to transmit this knowledge in a formulated scheme, but rather that the knowledge, by its very nature, defies the treatment of analysis and description. It exists "only in practice."

It is certainly true that when people engage in skilled activities there is a certain amount which they can learn from instructions supplied by others, whether these be supplied by the written or spoken word. It is also true that there is, beyond this, a certain amount which can only be gained by actual experience of the activity. This is the part we speak of when we talk about "learning from practice." One of the characteristics of a skill is that there is a clearly defined aim which delineates it from other activities. There is a conventional target which participants are expected to aim for if they are engaging in the activity, and which will be used as a standard against which their performance will be judged. The two types of knowledge, technical and practical, are designed to assist in the achievement (or nearer approach) of the conventional target. In golf, for example, the conventional target is to complete the eighteen holes of the course by using as few strokes as possible; and this aim is assisted by both the technical knowledge (of which clubs to use, how to stand, etc.) and the practical knowledge (of how much force to apply, when and how to swing the hips, and so on).

Participation in a skilled activity consists in an attempt to perform actions which will modify the observed universe to a predetermined pattern. The conventional target tells us how the observed universe should appear after we have performed the action, and thus gives us an ideal state against which we can measure the actual modification achieved. When we embark on a twenty-foot putt on the green of a golf course, we know that the conventional target would have the observed universe different after our stroke—to the effect that the ball would be in the hole.[6] If, after our attempt, the ball *does* enter the hole, we can, by the standards of the conventional target, call our attempt successful. The conventional target may be absolute or it may be comparative, but its existence is essential to separate from other activities the limited field of a particular skill. In golf we have a theoretical absolute target, in that the ability to complete eighteen holes in eighteen strokes would be regarded as perfect by anyone who contemplated the activity. But in tennis the target is comparative, for we are only required to place the ball with such directions and velocities that our opponent cannot return it.

Of course, in many skills the achievement of the nominated objective is hedged about with artificially imposed limitations (rules of the game) in order to make its attainment more difficult, or to make comparative estimation of participants easier and fairer. These limitations become qualifications to the target, making it more limited. The objective in golf is thus to complete an eighteen-hole course in as few strokes as possible, while carrying no more than fourteen clubs of an approved design, while counting two penalty strokes for every shot out of bounds, and so forth. These imposed limitations are more evident in the skills we call sports, but can often be present in other skills. If a clarinetist, for example, were to introduce a wind machine which could be controlled electronically by switches, he would not, however satisfactory the performance, be described as a good player. The notion of a skilled clarinetist is one which assumes the limitation that the instrument must be played with the mouth.

It might be argued that in some activities—for example, playing musical instruments or painting pictures—there is no clearly defined target. The musician whose aim is to be "better" than anyone else does not necessarily know what standard will be used, and what performance he must achieve to be "better." This is true, and serves to demonstrate that there are facets of these activities which cannot be called "skill" at all. One of the criteria which distinguish a skill or a craft from an art is that the skill or craft has nominated standards by which it can be rated and that these standards have become "objectified" by their public formulation. The score in a game of golf is not a matter of subjective opinion, whereas the excellence of a musical recital most certainly is. This is not to say that musical appreciation must be entirely subjective. On the contrary, it is because there are clearly defined standards of measurement and assessment that musical appreciation is something which can be *taught:* people can be told what to look for and how to appreciate it. Nonetheless, there remains in the judgment of a musical performance an element which depends upon the reactions of the observer.

If there is in the minds of the participants or spectators of a pursuit a clearly defined objective which is independent of their individual opinions, then the activity may be described as a skill or a craft. If the achievement of success depends for its attainment on the response of the spectator, then we are dealing with an activity which has elements of "art" in it, as well as (possibly) skill. Many activities involve elements of both. A photograph can be a work of skill if it is to be only a likeness; people who inspect it can compare it with the subject and evaluate the accuracy of its representation. It can also, though, be a work of art if the contemplation of it evokes in the minds of spectators some awareness of the relationships between the subject, the photographer, and the photograph.

In consideration of skill, however, we are limited to those activities in which there is a nominated and clearly appreciated objective. We deal with cases in which the participant knows what it is he is trying to do, in which we might say that he has a mental picture of how the universe should look after a successful attempt has been made. The degree to which his performance produces a state corresponding to that mental picture represents the degree to which his performance can be called successful. The technical and practical knowledge are necessary components of the achievement of such a correspondence.

If we subject these components to a more detailed examination, we can see that the difference between them centers around the notion of their capacity to be universalized. Including in the category of knowledge which can be formulated all of that which is capable *in principle* of being formulated, we are left with that which never can be formulated, which concerns itself with individual capabilities in particular circumstances.[7] This knowledge can never be formulated into general rules because there are no general rules about it. People vary so much in their capabilities and in the ways in which they react to particular circumstances that they can be guided by the experience of others to only a limited extent. Science is independent of the individual in one sense, because its tests can, in principle, be repeated at any time by anyone, and with the expectation of the same result. In the case of a specific human performance we do not expect the same result, simply because we know people are different. The physical limitations of one man might make him incapable of exactly reproducing the technique devised by another to achieve a specific purpose. This is the major variable in human performance, which cannot be resolved to a set of general rules; it involves a necessary dependence on the individual.

In addition to learning the knowledge which is general, which applies to everyone who engages in the activity, there is the extra knowledge to be learned which applies only to the individual case. The technical knowledge is that which is pitched at a level sufficiently low that the individual differences between people are not an intruding factor. The practical knowledge is knowledge gained above that level, where information relates to the individual case only. There are general rules in every activity, rules which will help the learner by quickly supplying him with knowledge that applies to everyone who undertakes the activity. In the absence of such rules, a participant might educate himself by a long process of testing different attempts and rejecting those which produce less adequate results than other attempts. But this is an unnecessarily long process when the knowledge may be gained from the many experiences of other participants and communicated through a book or through the mouth of an instructor.

For practical knowledge, however, the participant has no alternative to discovering it for himself. He cannot learn it from others because it does not apply to others. It is knowledge which concerns itself with such factors as the individual's sensory equipment, his muscular responses, the sensitivity of his nerve endings. These are factors about which we can say that the knowledge of one individual about himself not only cannot be communicated to others, but that it would be of no value to others since it would be knowledge which did not apply to them. They must learn for themselves the *equivalent* knowledge concerning their own sensory equipment, muscular responses, and sensitivity of nerve endings.

Oakeshott says that this practical knowledge can "neither be taught nor learned, but only imparted and acquired. . . . and the *only* way to acquire it is by apprenticeship to a master—not because the master can teach it (he cannot), but because it can be acquired *only* by continuous contact with one who is perpetually practising it."[8] By his use of these terms Oakeshott gives the impression that the practical knowledge is possessed by one person (the master) and "imparted" by him to another (the apprentice).

From the previous argument I would regard this as a fundamentally erroneous and deceptive way of looking at the problem. My contention is that the apprentice is not attempting to learn something which the master already knows but is attempting to learn for himself the equivalent knowledge which will apply to him personally. This is knowledge which the master does *not* already have, and cannot, therefore, "impart." The master knows his own abilities and limitations, in addition to the general rules of the operation which apply to everyone undertaking it. The apprentice knows only the general rules, and is seeking to acquire not the extra knowledge about the master's abilities and limitations but new knowledge concerning his own.[9]

The point is important because it enables us to see how the knowledge is gained, and how progress is thus made toward closer achievement of whatever end it is that delineates the activity. All of the knowledge requisite to a good performance *can* be gained by testing proposed attempts and eliminating those that are less adequate than others. But since a good part of the information is general in nature (the technical knowledge), it is easier and quicker to obtain it from secondary sources, even though we appreciate that somewhere along the line it had to be acquired by someone through testing against alternatives. The nongeneral knowledge, that which relates only to one person (the practical knowledge), must be gained by himself because no one else knows it.

If we now consider a novice in the process of acquiring a particular skill, we can inspect the various stages of his progress. Having learned what are the nominated objectives and the limitations imposed on his performance, he will read instruction books on the subject or take lessons from a coach. Having mastered the technical knowledge, no one supposes that he will be a competent performer, for he still has to acquire the practical knowledge. The time comes when he must make his first attempt, and compare its result with what should have happened had he been successful. The feedback in skills is usually of the direct kind, which not only tells us that an attempt was inadequate but indicates to us the respects and the degree to which it was so. The learner makes a new attempt on the basis of that first result, and will, if he approaches nearer the conventional objective, reject the way he tried the first time. Learning through practice might be a long process, especially where highly complex and subtle skills are sought, but it is universally agreed to be necessary if one is to achieve improved proficiency.

Progress in the acquisition of skills is governed by the two-part analysis given in the chapter on science.[10] If the objective is agreed upon, progress comes about as the less adequate competing attempts are eliminated in critical trials. Unlike scientific activity, though, the attempts are in the form of behavioral performances rather than proposed models, and only part of the knowledge gained is applicable to others. There are thus facets of skill acquisition in which progress will be specific to the individual and in which an advance will not necessarily benefit other participants. An advance in science, when it is publicized, increases the ability of everyone to predict the observed universe. An advance in golf by an individual might not be susceptible to publication and might benefit no one but the person who made it, if it falls into the class of knowledge which applies only to himself.

A curious effect of such advances in skill is that even though the achievement is individual, and even though the particular advance is inaccessible and inapplicable to anyone else, such advances can nevertheless bring about improvement in the performance of others. The discussion thus far has used terms such as *adequate performance* and *successful attempts,* without going into the detail of how far toward a theoretical possible achievement people attempt to reach. Research on skill, performed under laboratory conditions, has shown two interesting results: the level of adequacy is apparently determined by both the participant's estimate of his own capabilities and the knowledge of what is required of him.

H. Helson advances the hypothesis, in his *Adaptation-Level Theory,*[11] that individuals set for themselves a standard of performance which they are content to reach, and which is habitually set below the level of performance they actually are capable of achieving. Fitts and Posner, in their *Human Perfor-*

mance,[12] claim that the "most widely accepted generalization from experiments concerning this issue (Cofer and Appley, 1964)[13] is that successful performance leads to an increase in the standard of excellence, while failure leads to a decrease. There can be exceptions—for example, when long-continued success leads to boredom with a task and unwillingness to expend additional effort." But they go on to show that level of performance can be varied according to whether or not the task is arranged to suggest that a high level of performance is expected. They quote Mace (1953)[14] as saying that improved performance in an aiming task is achieved simply by adding more concentric rings within the established periphery, thus making what previously appeared to be good performance look mediocre.

While it is evident that attempts to attain an ideal objective might be subject to practical limitations, such as lack of strength or dexterity, that will set the theoretically possible attainment well below the ideal, it appears that the subject's estimate of his capabilities is usually set below that theoretical limit. When it is clear that more is expected, more is supplied. It comes about, therefore, that an advance by one participant, even though the knowledge required to achieve it might be peculiar to himself, can nonetheless promote improved performance in others by letting them know that more is possible.

It is claimed that men can now run four-minute mile races because of better diet and better health. All this may be true, but it ignores the ingredient of motivation. When Roger Bannister ran the first four-minute mile, other runners raised their sights to what they saw was now a possible attainment, and within a very short time many of them proved capable of achieving the new target. Just as we value the innovator in science who sees new problems or proposes new models, so do we value the innovator in skilled activity who shows us new standards to be sought. Societies may continue for many generations to perform particular activities in traditional

Trial and Error

ways, not because they are incapable of achieving better but often because they do not appreciate that this is possible.

An important function of the "master" in acquisition of skill by an "apprentice" is that his achievements enable that apprentice to set his sight to the level of achievement required. By continually showing what is possible, the master is a source of encouragement in the improvement of the apprentice. Oakeshott is too restrictive when he says that practical knowledge is *only* acquired by apprenticeship, and *only* by continuous contact with those in constant practice. As has been indicated, the learner might hope to acquire this knowledge as a result of his own trials. In Oakeshott's model there is no accounting for the self-taught, no explanation of the popular sentimental theme of the gypsy who has managed, without training, to become a brilliant guitarist. The master increases the ease and the rapidity of the student's progress. Not only do his achievements supply conception of an appropriate target, but his work supplies feedback to the student who can compare it with his own. The student can greatly restrict the range of his first conjectures by watching the master, and has a constant comparison between his own work and that of a successful performer. By working alongside him, the student is attempting to gain sufficient information about himself to be able to duplicate the *effects* of the master's actions.[15]

But more knowledge is gained in the doing than in the watching. Anyone who professes a fair proficiency at any particular skill will confirm that there is such a thing as the right "feel" to a performance. The baker, making his dough, has done it so often that he has acquired enough feedback from previous trials to estimate when his dough "feels" right. He has observed the result of baking dough of various consistencies so many times that he has come to know what to expect from a dough of a particular texture or elasticity. This is the type of knowledge which comes only from experience, for while (in this case) a certain amount of knowledge could be acquired by watching an expert over a long period, much more direct feedback is gained when one's own hands are in the mixture, feeling its temperature and consistency, as well as merely seeing what it looks like. A golfer, playing a tee shot, comes to know the feeling he receives through the club shaft when his drive is a good, clean one. In almost any skilled activity the expert is able to make decisions and to assess his performance *before* the result of his activity is known, and with an accuracy which seems almost mystic to a beginner. But the beginner, too, given sufficient trials, can hope to accumulate the information appropriate to this level of proficiency.

In general, the more augmented the feedback, the greater the progress in performance. Since the method requires the constant selection of the more adequate over the less adequate, then more information will usually improve the efficiency of the decision-making process and will increase ability to bring proposed alternatives to a crisis point at which we can make a preference judgment based on their performance.

The dramatic increase in performance which can result from augmented feedback has been demonstrated under trial. After the chance discovery that subjects improved their performance in laboratory tests when a noisy clock was present (providing audible information about the passage of time), Alfred Smode[16] investigated the effect in detail. In skill experiments, where the nominated objective was to keep a randomly varying needle centered by rotating a dial, Smode allowed some groups to be told, after the end of a trial, what their performance had been and allowed other groups to see this performance continuously recorded on a counter. The differences in performance were striking. The four groups with "normal" feedback improved over a dozen trials, from being on target 40 percent of the time to achieving 50 percent on-target performance. The four groups with "augmented" feed-

Trial and Error

back started with nearly 50 percent success and improved it, over the same period, to 64 percent success.

Commenting on Smode's results, Fitts and Posner suggest that because the performance of the augmented feedback groups was better even for the first trial, increased motivation occurred. They advance the idea that the subjects were "motivated to work harder" by the success-counter, and that improvement from the very first trial reveals this. While this is by no means clear, since the subjects were apparently receiving feedback *during* the very first trial and were in a position to gain immediate benefit from it, it is a possible explanation for the improvement in performance, and (as Fitts and Posner point out) still leaves the question whether the group with augmented feedback had actually learned more. Fortunately, the same point occurred to Smode, for he repeated his experiments with the same groups, this time withdrawing the augmented feedback from half of the group which had been given it in the first series of trials and retaining it for the other half, while similarly dividing the group which had not enjoyed the augmented feedback into two sections, half of them now receiving the augmented feedback. The groups which had received augmented feedback on the first day showed better performance than the other groups, *whether or not* they continued to receive the additional feedback. The implication is clear: these groups gained knowledge appropriate to improved performance when they received the augmented feedback, knowledge they subsequently retained even when conditions reverted to "normal."

Motivation is a factor in the conditions for progress in both part 1 and part 2.[17] Not only must there be agreement about the conventional objective, but people must actually engage in testing and inadequacy elimination before there can be progress. As was seen in the discussion of scientific activity, the motivation need not be directly related to the nominated

79

end. People might well engage in scientific research and become successful scientists without being motivated to increase man's ability to predict the observed universe. The important thing is that progress requires the real motivations to be served by achievement of the nominated objective. Whether the driving force be desire for gain, for admiration, or simply for the satisfaction derived by achieving a high standard in a chosen activity, it will be conducive to progress in any field if it can be directed toward the declared objective of that field.

Many of the activities which we describe as skills are so arbitrary in their nominated ends that no one could possibly wish to achieve the objectives for their own sake. They are "conventional targets" in that society decides, by convention, to reward a good performance by substance or by esteem. It is difficult to imagine why anyone should wish to use specially shaped clubs to hit a small white ball into a hole several hundred yards away—difficult, that is, to imagine anyone wishing to do this for its own sake. But because society has made this, by convention, a "test of skill," people are enabled to fulfill other desires by its accomplishment. Self-gratification, fame, and fortune can all be fulfilled by excellence at golf because society has set it as a standard test.

At a more serious level, society can, by conventional decision, direct the motives of its members into the service of a nominated target which might have, in itself, a very low potential for motivation. Charitable organizations, despite their stress on the morality of charitable donation, nonetheless take care to ensure that other motives can be fulfilled by the achievement of *their* ends. Often their advertising is directed in such a way that people can absolve guilty consciences, can feel the warm glow of self-satisfaction, by contributing to an end which the organization sets but which has low power to motivate individuals outside the organization. Some religions, while stressing the value of moral goodness as service to the divinity, also take care to hedge it about with rewards of eternal life and divine favor, so that it becomes a target for more self-seeking motivations.

Whatever the actual motivation, it is enough for improvement in a skilled activity that the subject accept its nominated aim as a way of achieving his own objectives. Given this, the subject can apply the technique of testing comparatively and eliminating inferior alternatives. The fact that a large body of what he would discover by this method is of such a general nature that it is susceptible of wide application means that he is able to take the short cut of obtaining some of his information from secondary sources. The rest of the knowledge he needs in order to improve his abilities must be learned by himself because it applies only to himself.

We can see that, in discovering and extending their abilities, each generation must start from a common pool of communicable knowledge which applies to all. Through practice they acquire, individually, an extension of knowledge in the activity which applies only to themselves, and which endures only for their lifetimes; each generation must start afresh from the common pool. Concern for an increase in the knowledge and abilities of the human race must therefore take the form of concern for enlargement and extension of that common pool. While the man who achieves a previously unrivaled performance in any skill is esteemed and valued in his own time, it is the man who achieves improvement in the *technical* knowledge of an activity, he who gains an advance that everyone can partake of, who is awarded the more lasting acclaim of posterity.

In one of the exquisite footnotes which adorn his work, Michael Oakeshott tells of the wheelwright who criticizes the duke for reading, expressing the sentiment (which Oakeshott plainly approves of) that "in my opinion it must have been the same with the men of old. All that was worth handing on, died with them; the rest they put in their books. That is why I said that what you were reading was the lees and scum of bygone men."[18] The valuation is here placed upon practical knowledge; it is what a man achieves of his potential in a lifetime. Following from our previous argument, though, we reverse the valuation. What they put in their books was what they discovered that was of general application; what died with them was knowledge which applied only to themselves and which was therefore of no use to anyone else. One can look at the former as their "lees and scum," but from the point of view of the human race and its desire to extend its knowledge and capabilities, one could regard what was left as part of the distilled essence of progress.

Notes

[1] Michael Oakeshott, *Rationalism in Politics* (1962), p. 7. The first essay, of the same title as the book, dates from 1947.

[2] Ibid., p. 8.

[3] Ibid., p. 11.

[4] Ibid., p. 8.

[5] Ibid., p. 11.

[6] This analysis does not imply that people consciously go through the procedure of imagining how the universe will look after their attempt has succeeded. It remains true, however, that the difference between ideal and actual achievement represents the shortfall of the attempt.

[7] In Oakeshott's footnote (pp. 9 and 10 of the essay "Rationalism in Politics") referred to at the end of this chapter, the wheelwright says: "The right pace, neither slow nor fast, cannot get into the hand unless it comes from the heart. It is a thing that cannot be put into words [rules]; there is an art in it that I cannot explain to my son."

[8] Oakeshott, op. cit., p. 11 (my italics).

[9] This is the crucial point. If the knowledge is not "imparted and acquired" by a process of transference, but gained by the individual from his own trials and errors, then the element of irrationality and mystery is removed.

[10] Ch. 2.

[11] H. Helson, *Adaptation-Level Theory* (1964).

[12] Paul M. Fitts and Michael I. Posner, *Human Performance* (1967), ch. 3, "Motivation and Performance."

[13] C. N. Cofer and M. H. Appley, *Motivation: Theory and Research* (1964).

[14] C. A. Mace, "Homeostasis, Needs and Values," *British Journal of Psychology* (1953).

[15] This is similar to a point made by W. V. Quine. The composition may be different within, so long as the finished effect is the same. When one is cutting bushes to the shape of animals, two bushes may be given a very similar appearance, despite their widely different internal structures.

[16] A. Smode, "Learning and Performance in a Tracking Task under Two Levels of Achievement Information Feedback," *Journal of Experimental Psychology* (1958).

[17] Ch. 2.

[18] Oakeshott, op. cit., n. pp. 9 and 10.

5
History & the Study of Mankind

Problems are encountered in the attempt to apply the two-part equation of progress to the disciplines which make mankind the special object of their study. History and the social sciences cannot be subsumed under the general heading "scientific activity" because they are concerned with the orderly and systematic presentation of purported facts related by subject matter. As W. H. Walsh[1] points out, such a description would include a railway timetable. To show that the equation applies to progress in these fields, it is necessary to show (1) that there is an agreed-upon and accepted aim of the activity and (2) that steps toward the fulfillment of that aim are taken by innovative proposal, testing comparatively (so that a preference decision can be taken at a crisis point as to which proposal most adequately fulfills the aim), and retention of that proposal pending further competitive testing.

It is convenient to take history as an example of the "studies of mankind" because it is a discipline sufficiently broad to allow the social sciences to be included as subsets, governed by rules which are similar in their essentials.[2] By the use of the term *history* we intend to denote the activity of the men and women who have made the doings of the human race the particular object of their attention, and not merely the activity in which our species has engaged (which is also described as "history"). For more than a century there has been close debate concerning what is, or should be, the object of their exercise; about the methods used by historians; and whether it is correct to describe history as a "scientific" activity. This is not surprising. The books of the Old Testament bear witness to the antiquity of the discipline, and it is natural that men should have speculated about what it is they are doing when they are engaged in what is called historical activity.

An immediate problem which arises when one attempts an analysis and summary description of what is involved in the study of history is that our concept of what constitutes the activity has been sufficiently vague as to admit a whole range of different pursuits under the one heading. This discussion is limited to dealing with those historians who engage in *explanation,* rather than simple *narration* (a limitation which still includes the activity of social scientists). A historian, for this purpose, shall be taken to mean someone who tries to build up a coherent picture of the past by telling us what he thinks happened and *why it happened.* The justification for this is simple enough, though some historians might not care to admit it. It is that those engaged in the study and appreciation of history tend to say that while the mere narration of events is a legitimate historical activity, the intellectual exercise that consists in dealing with and interpreting these events is of a higher order, and constitutes much more the value of the operation.[3]

Just as we value more highly the scientist who sees the problem and makes an inventive proposal to solve it than those who pursue the more limited (albeit legitimately scientific) activity of compiling observational data, so in history do we value those who attempt to enlarge our understanding by asking questions of the "how" and "why" variety. It remains true that the delight in gossip we can observe in ourselves and our fellow creatures seems basic to mankind. There may

Trial and Error

always be historians who satisfy this urge of ours with highly readable and interesting accounts of what has happened in bygone ages. We shall still take pleasure in listening to the tales of the twelve Caesars, or of the love life of Napoleon; and no doubt this will continue to be described as "history." Doubtless, too, we shall continue to read, and to watch, accounts of popularized science, and to regard *The Wonders of the Heavens* as a "scientific" book. But in an examination of the role and function of the inquiry, we must give our interest primarily to those who would tell us, in history, *why* it happened as they think it did and to those who would tell us, in science, *why* it happens as they think it must.[4]

There is an immediate and obvious difference in the subject matter of science and of history which springs to mind as a possible objection to the treatment of them as branches of the same activity. Whereas science is concerned essentially with that which is repeatable, history occupies itself with a unique past which, once departed, may return no more. In science we postulate general laws which may constantly be tested; in history we explain one section of the past, contenting ourselves, for the most part, with a particular set of individual events.

While this might seem to place an impossible barrier forever between the two disciplines, if we examine more closely some of the activities which we describe as science we find among the numerous studies which come under that heading some which are subject to similar conditions. Geology, for example, is recognized as a legitimate branch of science, and yet it, too, concerns itself with the explanation and interpretation of events in the dead past. We might, it is true, argue that the postulates of geology are such that if we could duplicate the conditions which existed on earth millions of years ago, we would expect the same things to happen again. But the same might be said of history or the social sciences. We might expect there, too, that if we could repeat all the circumstances surrounding a particular civilization, we would find it following the same patterns again. In terms of content matter, then, there seems to be no reason to assign to history a status different from that which we award geology; but we may be wrong to consider geology as a science.

It might be argued that a geologist draws on general laws concerning the behavior of matter and applies them in a scientific way to the events with which his discipline is particularly concerned. The question whether the historian or social scientist applies "sociohistorical" laws governing the behavior of people and society to the specific events under study is a contentious one. Some historians have argued that these so-called laws are hardly to be found in the pages of history writing, and that historians do not use a scientific method of explanation.[5]

On the other side, the groups led by Popper and Hempel have argued, with more success, that explanation must *necessarily* involve reference to general laws. Popper alleges that the function of explanation is only fulfilled (in history as in science) if there is a combination of initial conditions and covering law.[6] The covering law is a conjecture, a tested but as yet unrejected proposition concerning what happens in the general case; the initial conditions are those which show that the particular example under consideration does indeed fall within the ambit of the general rule. In his example[7] we are invited to consider a string which breaks when a weight is attached. The fact that "the string broke" is explained by two statements: (1) "For this thread the characteristic maximum tension at which it is liable to break is equal to a one-pound weight" and (2) "The weight put on this thread was a two-pound weight." Statement 1 sets out the covering law, while 2 describes the initial conditions. Together they constitute an explanation.

It is difficult to confute an argument on so firm a ground in classical logic. Popper's "explanation" derives from the unarguable syllogism: (1) Every A is B; (2) X is an A;

(3) Therefore X is B. The conclusion, "Therefore X is B," follows completely and irrefutably from the premises (1 and 2).

Historians, it is argued, go through a similar process when presenting explanations; and the reason why the covering law is often not given is that it is frequently of a trivial, obvious nature and is implied rather than stated. Thus while a historian might say that an explanation of the form "Disraeli's death was caused by bronchial pneumonia" does not involve covering laws, one can show that, for this to be an acceptable explanation, it must be separated into two statements of the type suggested by Popper. It is no explanation at all unless we can take it that bronchial pneumonia causes death at times and that, for Disraeli, this was one of those times. In this case we might say (1) People who contract pneumonia when in a certain stage of weakness will die, and (2) Disraeli contracted pneumonia while in that stage of weakness.

Of course, it would be infinitely tedious and unnecessary to have this procedure spelled out every time. Most of the covering laws are so trivially obvious that no one would require this. It helps, nonetheless, if we appreciate the process when we come to deal with explanations involving laws which are neither obvious nor trivial. There are, it should be said, both historians and philosophers who assert that there are no complex laws, and that writers of history must be forever confined to the trivially obvious. It is argued that the facts involved for human beings and their societies are so numerous and so complicated that no one can ever hope to know enough about any one issue, much less postulate a general law. As adherents of this viewpoint are not loath to point out, there are precious few "laws of history" beyond the trivially obvious which have been suggested so far.[8] They further argue that the very uniqueness of historical events militates against the discovery of generalizations, that each historical situation has too many relevant and interconnected strands for it ever to be treated as if it were of a kind with any other, and that human behavior will always have far more causative factors than can ever be isolated or defined.

The difficulties apparent in predicting the behavior of any individual add weight to these arguments, but they do not preclude a scientific approach to history. A scientist, after all, is often unable to predict the behavior of a single atom; yet he can make valid predictions concerning the fate of large numbers of atoms. For an unstable isotope with a half-life of ninety-nine years, the physicist cannot tell us which atoms will decay first; but he can tell us that after ninety-nine years half of them will have gone. F. A. von Hayek, in his treatment of "orders of complexity,"[9] has shown that one can hope to produce pattern generalizations even where the behavior of human beings is concerned—even though one can never hope to know all of the highly complex details. The pattern generalization stops short at the point where the individual and indeterminate details of each particular case cause it to diverge from a predictable model. Thus the scientist who is engaged in the study of crystal formation may never be able to know all the facts about his chemicals and their circumstances to tell us what size his crystals will be; he may, nonetheless, know enough to be able to tell us that they will all be hexagonal.[10] In the same way, we might be able to recognize common patterns in historical events and be able to postulate pattern generalizations based on factors which are common to these events.

Each shipwreck is a unique event. When each ship has sunk and drowned its quota of passengers, there is an end of it. We will never again have a ship of the same size, the same structural stress patterns, carrying the same passengers in the same tidal conditions. We might notice though, from a series of such disasters, that passengers who are in the water and within (say) twenty yards of a sinking ship when it goes down tend to be sucked under and drowned. Even if we never have the technical skill required to measure all the tidal currents and eddies involved in the drowning of any one passenger, we can, despite this, make the perfectly reasonable generalization. Thus when we are asked "Why was Mr. X drowned?" a two-part answer, consisting of initial conditions and covering law, could be supplied. We might say in this case (1) Passengers within twenty yards of a sinking ship are usually sucked under and drowned as it goes down and (2) Mr. X was within twenty yards of the ship as it went down. We accept this as a satisfactory explanation of (3): Mr. X was drowned.

It would appear, therefore, that in spite of the number and complexity of factors in sociohistorical events, we can hope to supply general laws. In history we might postulate, after consideration of many revolutions, some such generalization as "In predominantly agrarian societies, revolution is usually preceded by certain successive stages of peasant discontent," and we might compose an index by which those "certain successive stages" could be measured. Even though such a thing as "peasant discontent" might never be quantifiable in detail, this fact does not render the postulated generalization useless. Professional historians are highly skilled at detecting signs of such things as peasant discontent. They might find evidence of it that other observers would either miss or not think of looking for. By imposing an arbitrary index, they might be able to measure the scale or degree to which discontent is present at various stages. Nonpayment of taxes is one stage, but clearly the resort to emigration from the land or sporadic acts of violence are others. Historians might, by recognizing the presence of factors which often precede a revolution, gain greater understanding of the period in question. If we inspect their work, we can see that many of them postulate such generalizations and make use of them in explanation.

However, a major difference is apparent between history and science in terms of the ability to predict. The method of innovative proposal and comparative testing has as one of its central pivots the use of experiment to check prediction against observation and thus to eliminate inadequacies systematically. When the scientist makes his generalization, he can usually set up trials to see it in action and can predict what will be observed, given certain known circumstances. The historian, however, is working with people and cannot set up experiments to see if his generalizations may be inspected at work; nor can he *predict* events about a past which is already dead and gone, and which is his principal field of study.[11]

Yet there is a historical *equivalent* of prediction, an equivalent which serves the same role as prediction does in science. True, a historian cannot set up controlled experiments with colonies of people to see if they behave as his generalizations say they should, but he can look at societies which have already existed, and look for things *which no one has previously thought of looking for*. He cannot make "predictions" about a dead past, but he can postulate things which ought to have happened and *then* look for evidence of them. This process of "retrodiction" has as its basis of validity that people must be looking for something not already known.[12] If, in light of a theory, some new factor is looked for and found, people praise the theory in the same way they praise a scientific theory which enables a successful prediction to be made. The substitution of retrodiction for prediction is allowed because we may be just as ignorant concerning a past event as we are about a future event. The new information, be it about what happens or what happened, serves to show us if our theory should be rejected or retained for the time being. In both science and history it can cause the modification or abandonment of the theory. This is what is meant by saying that retrodiction serves the same role: we mean that it provides a mechanism whereby the method of innovative proposal and comparative testing may be operated.

We may take the secondary aim of historical activity to be the understanding and explanation of man's activities, even

Trial and Error

though we might care to advance a higher end that is served by this secondary aim. It was suggested, for scientific activity, that the aim conventionally set for increasing our ability to predict the world of our observation might actually serve a desire to *control,* to so order the universe that it conforms more to our desires and renders us less vulnerable to the random hazards which might be encountered. Similarly in history, it is possible that our attempts at understanding and explanation are less dispassionate than they seem, and that E. H. Carr[13] is correct to say that our aim is to do something about it, to learn enough about the nature of man and his societies to enable us to order the world of civil life much more to our satisfaction. Whether or not the "name of the game" here, too, is power, we can accept that the secondary aim of understanding and explanation can be approached systematically by choice between competing proposals, provided we are in possession of a technique which gives us grounds for choice. Retrodiction supplies that technique. Possession of a set of generalizations with initial conditions fulfills the function of explanation; while the generalizations proposed can be tested against each other by establishing whether the outcomes expected to follow from the initial conditions have left historical evidence of their occurrence.

If, in our previous example, one did indeed postulate that "in agrarian societies, revolution is usually preceded by certain successive stages of peasant discontent," and if one then looked at an example of a revolution in an agrarian society *not previously considered* for this aspect, and if one found evidence of the successive stages of discontent postulated by the generalization, then the theory could rightly be considered a useful one. The obvious caution is that the historian finds what he is looking for in a *new* field, and does not merely use existing knowledge to support his preconceived ideas. If the historian has already inspected *all* agrarian-society revolutions before making his conjecture, he can hardly test his idea by examining a previously unconsidered case; rather he would have to test it by deducing implications which have *not* been examined in the societies he knows about. Provided the exercise is pursued honestly, retrodiction fulfills the same function in history that prediction does in science. And there are limited fields of science, such as geology and evolutionary biology, in which retrodiction in this manner plays a larger role than normal prediction. Any field of study which sets as one of its tasks the accounting for a present state of affairs through an understanding and explanation of a unique past must necessarily find that retrodiction plays the major role in any preference decisions concerning competing proposed generalizations.

Even though generalizations can be formulated in the study of history, and even though they can be competitively tested, they must be inspected to see if they are of the same form as scientific propositions before one can establish that the study of history proceeds by similar methods. Our scientific conjectures, we saw, are often cast in the form "Whenever X, then Y," but if we look again at the examples of the type of conjecture to be expected in history, we meet such terms as *tend, possible, usually,* and the like. We note that all these terms imply considerably less certainty than we find in scientific postulates, and we are led to ask what kind of "general law" is it which does not apply to all instances. Is it not nonsense to speak of a generalization which is not, in fact, general? Of what value is it for us to realize that something *might* happen? Surely we should be concerned with what *must* happen?

The answer to these points is that in sociohistorical laws we enter the realms of probability. Human beings and their societies are infinitely more complex than weights and wires or falling bodies. One two-pound weight resembles another two-pound weight to a much greater extent than one human being can ever resemble another; the number of variables is less. When we attempt to conjecture how human beings in groups will behave under different conditions, we come up against the practical limit of the number of variables we can know about and manipulate simultaneously. Our "laws," therefore, account for the behavior of men and women only to a very primitive level, below which the individual characteristics of our subjects make no difference. Beyond that level is a range in which our laws apply to most, then to many, to some, and to few.

Most human characteristics follow a Gaussian curve of distribution.[14] Not only physical characteristics, such as height and weight, but factors such as intelligence, too, are grouped under the bell-shaped curve. This means that while we cannot predict the characteristics of an individual, we can predict the distribution of characteristics for a group of individuals. We could not predict the height, weight, or intelligence quotient of any individual drawn at random from Western Europe, but we could draw a graph predicting the distribution of such characteristics for a thousand individuals drawn at random. It is not unreasonable to suppose that we could make statistical predictions concerning factors which depend upon human characteristics, even though we might not be able to specify which individuals these predictions would be fulfilled by.

To give an example of this we might put forward, as a general law, that all men die within a year if totally deprived of food and water. This is well below the primitive level, where individual physiology, capacity for endurance, and will to survive will be brought to bear. If, however, we set the figure at forty days, we would have to amend the law to read "*Most* men die if totally deprived of food and water for forty days," because we have reason to suppose that there might have been isolated cases of survival even after so long a period of deprivation. The point about probability is that while we know that only a very small number of people have such capacity for endurance that they could survive an ordeal of this nature, we do not know in advance which ones they will be. We can, when dealing with large numbers of people, make statistical estimates of a higher order of accuracy, but we cannot say in advance which particular individuals will fall on which side of whatever dividing lines are set for consideration. It is not true that there are no adequate causal factors to account for the behavior of the individual; it is just that they are beyond the range of measurement.

This consideration, while it limits the certain applicability of a generalization to any particular case, does not, I think, affect the validity of the generalization itself. It may still be tested and amended in the ways which have been described, and people may still find reasons for retaining or rejecting it. Where we come across a case which falls outside, we are not inclined to reject the generalization immediately, because we know it referred only to a probability. What we attempt to do is discover *why* this special case lies outside, in order that our original generalization might be made more rigorous. If we come across a man who was within twenty yards of a ship as it went down, and yet managed to avoid being drowned, we try to find out why: we try to locate the reasons for such odd exceptions in order that we might modify the original proposition in such a way that it takes account of them.

This is not to say that our generalizations of the sociohistorical variety cannot be shown inadequate by testing. On the contrary, being statistical predictions, they can be assailed statistically. The generalization that IQ distribution for mankind follows a Gaussian curve, irrespective of ethnic background, has been severely attacked by statistics which show that IQ scores, obtained by nonculturally loaded tests, group around different curves for different races.[15] And the generalization that the IQ score depends in large measure upon social background has been jolted by figures which show that both the North American Indian and the Mexican American score on higher curves than the North American

Trial and Error

Negro, even though the latter is socially advantaged to a considerable degree by comparison with the others.[16]

We see, then, that in the part of history which concerns itself with explanation, with the extension of knowledge and understanding, we have all the ingredients for the successful application of a method similar in its essentials to that pursued in science. We make our innovative proposals as we realize that there are questions which require answers (explanations), and we deduce what would follow as consequences of those proposals. We then use our elaborate techniques to examine new fields to see if the evidence corresponds to what our deduced consequences lead us to expect. If the evidence corresponds with our "retrodiction," we have reason for preferring the proposal over proposals which did not do this. In the absence of such a method, it would be difficult to conceive of reasons for choosing between two equally possible alternative explanations. We retain those explanations which our evidence does not belie.

History, like other disciplines, is a developing discipline. In history, as in science, we are less than satisfied with the methods used today and with the conclusions reached by previous generations of practitioners. It may be that we have a concept of the ideal approach, and that we recognize that there have been many who have not used it. It is pertinent to point out that previous works of history and science may still be appreciated on a different level, as literature, even though we recognize that their findings and perhaps their methods have been superseded. Both the scientific writings of Aristotle and the historical writings of Gibbon may remain immortal classics of art, even though we now admit that their value to the disciplines of science and history has declined.

Leaving aside the question of their value as art, I suggest that since history and science use a similar method in pursuit of similar aims, they could both be considered simply as branches of the search for knowledge. Our knowledge of history, like our knowledge of the universe, is an accumulation of unrejected propositions. To say that, because history deals with what is past, there must be some things which we can know for certain, is to overvalue the reliance we should place on the evidence of our (or other people's) senses. Logically speaking, we could be wrong about everything, even something as seemingly certain as, for example, "Napoleon commanded the defeated army at the Battle of Waterloo." Despite all the tests this suggestion passes (eyewitness accounts, his own writings, etc.), it is always logically possible that we are mistaken. An ingenious mind can readily think up hundreds of alternative possibilities—perhaps a double kidnaped Napoleon and took his place on the night before the battle. If any of these alternatives were testable, we might soon find them contradicted by other evidence (itself possibly misleading). Any alternatives which were untestable could be discarded, since we could never have reason to prefer them or reject them. As with science, it is more helpful to think in terms not of "correct" but of "most adequate." The suggestion which passes most tests, and is thus more consistent with the rest of what we interpret as the evidence, is retained as the most useful one.

To see this process in action, we might look at some of the great controversies of historical explanation. The Walcott thesis,[17] postulating that personal and family groups dominated the politics of the reign of Queen Anne far more than ideological differences, was challenged by other historians who used methods modeled on the outline given here. They devised tests based on the deducible implications of the Walcott theory, inspected new fields for evidence, and found the original suggestion very poor at retrodiction. Holmes, Speck, and Dickinson all found that the "personal and family groups" voted what was practically a straight ticket on the ideological issues. Division lists from parliamentary records display a remarkable ideological consistency. The ideological conflict can be seen right down to individual constituencies, through private letters and estate or church records. These tests have all pointed to the rejection (or at least the severe modification) of the theory. A useful result of Walcott's innovative proposal is that we now have a much clearer idea of what England was like in the reign of Queen Anne. We realize that the ideological conflicts divided all classes of society much more than was previously thought possible.

Another such debate concerns the Rise of the Gentry issue,[18] the postulate that the English civil war and political instability must be seen against the background of a rising gentry challenging the old, and declining, aristocracy. Challengers of the theory, and its defenders, set to work on a highly detailed examination of the economic changes among and within the classes, and tested the expected consequences of the theory. Again, a severe modification has resulted. Evidence that by the 1630s the aristocracy had succeeded in maintaining its position means that the suggestion cannot be accepted in its simple form.

Both of these examples illustrate that historians use the technique of competitive testing (and show us, too, that a theory can be useful in history if it generates tests, even though it may itself be discarded). The various subdisciplines within history, such as dating, documentation, etc., are used in a scientific way to establish tests on the proposals which concern evidence or explanations. It would appear that history can be treated as a science such as geology, concerned with the formulation of general laws and with the application of those laws to provide explanations for specific and nonrepeatable events. Progress in history, like progress in science, proceeds as a result of choices, made after testing at a crisis point, to reject some suggestions but to retain others. The progress is toward understanding and explanation, and is made because each testing choice at a crisis point is made on the ability of proposals under consideration to help us achieve precisely those ends. It is testing and retrodiction which enable us to proceed toward the establishment of ever more adequate general laws and initial conditions, whose combination serves the function of explanation. Progress in the former, by application of our two-part formula, necessarily involves progress in the latter.

Explanation in history, as in science, derives from the combination of (1) covering law and (2) initial conditions. Historians who have attempted to claim a unique status for the study of history have perhaps been misled by the peculiar emphasis of their discipline. It is true that history concerns itself with the individual case rather than the general rule, and that historians tend to write about the French Revolution or the Russian Revolution rather than revolution in general. But none of this alters the logical structure of their explanations.

In many sciences the initial conditions are only used in the attempt to establish general laws. They are, in a sense, trivial. They constitute the conditions of an experiment which is designed to put the general law to test. History reverses the focus. With the same logical structure to its explanations, history uses the general laws in order to establish the initial conditions. It is the initial conditions, the specific cases, which interest historians; and it is these to which their attention is given.

The fact that many sciences concentrate their emphasis on the general laws, whereas history usually concentrates on the initial conditions, should not lead us into making an artificial distinction between the two. The sciences which I compared to history, namely geology and evolutionary biology, are ones which often take the historian's focus on particular cases. In both of them the general laws are often used to explain and account for a variety of initial conditions which have occurred. If both of them are to be regarded as legitimate fields for the exercise of scientific activity, then the special emphasis of history need not exclude it from similar classification. In the final analysis, however, the labels are unimportant. What matters is that the study of history can progress through conjecture and competitive testing toward a nearer approach to the aim of the activity.

Notes

[1] W. H. Walsh, *An Introduction to the Philosophy of History* (1951), ch. 2.

[2] The term *history* is taken here in such a way that the behavior of man in society is part of its field of study. From the "explanatory" view of history (taken below), the work of the social sciences may be seen as building some of the blocks from which a historical explanation is built.

[3] Thus while Robert Blake, in *The Conservative Party from Peel to Churchill* (1970), can say, "History is not an exact science, and it never will be. It is a good story," his own work belies so simple a view. He attempts at every stage to offer explanations of unique events in terms of generalizations applied to particular cases. In the work cited, for example, he makes use more than once of a proposed generalization that conservative parties perform better in elections when they do not propose radical policies. He advances the view that if electors want radicalism, they vote for a radical party, and he uses this generalization to account for some Conservative defeats. Clearly, his own writing is far more than the telling of "a good story."

[4] It is worth noting, in this connection, that eminence in the two disciplines has been reserved for those who engage in this type of activity.

[5] H. A. L. Fisher, for example, says in his *History of Europe* (1935): "These harmonies are concealed from me. I can see only one emergency following upon another as wave follows upon wave, only one great fact with respect to which, since it is unique, there can be no generalisations, only one safe rule for the historian: that he should recognise in the development of human destinies the play of the contingent and the unforeseen."

⁶Sir Karl Popper, *The Open Society and Its Enemies* (1945), vol. II, ch. 25.

⁷Ibid.

⁸Whereas it might be argued on the other side that the search for such laws is comparatively recent, and that further study might well reveal more of them.

⁹F. A. von Hayek, *Studies in Philosophy, Politics and Economics* (1967).

¹⁰Hayek's example, from the work cited.

¹¹The social sciences face an even more serious drawback. As with history, they suffer from the moral impossibility of setting up societies in order to test theories. In making predictions concerning already existing societies, they encounter three problems:

(1) The social scientist is also a citizen, and has responsibilities to his fellow men. He might not wish to keep quiet about unpleasant consequences which have been predicted *and which can be averted.*

(2) His predictions might therefore be self-negating. The making and announcement of the prediction might serve to prevent its coming about.

(3) His predictions might be self-fulfilling. A prediction that a certain bank will soon collapse might be sufficient to persuade people to withdraw funds, and hence precipitate the very collapse which was predicted.

All of these are severe restrictions to the award of genuine scientific status to the social sciences.

¹²The use of known information to "corroborate" a theory must, however, be viewed with caution. Footnote 13 of chapter 3 illustrates the dangers.

¹³In *What Is History?*, E. H. Carr says: "And when we recognised certain explanations as rational, and other explanations as not rational, we were, I suggest, distinguishing between explanations which served some end and explanations which did not."

Carr is using the example of a road accident, pointing out that we only seize on causes about which we can hope to do something. The fact that the victim was crossing the road to buy cigarettes does not mean that cigarettes have to be regarded as a contributing factor. We can do something about drunken drivers, about faulty brakes, and about road siting; we cannot reduce road fatalities by acting against cigarette smoking.

[14] A Gaussian curve is a graph obtained by plotting particular values of the measured characteristic along the horizontal axis, against the numbers of cases with those particular values along the vertical axis. In the so-called normal distribution, this graph takes the form of a bell-shaped curve, with most cases clustering under the bell about the mean value and very few examples of high or low values under the lip of the bell, either at the right or left.

[15] A. R. Jensen et al., *Environment, Heredity and Intelligence* (1969), Harvard Reprint Series No. 2.

[16] The implications of these figures (and their limitations) are dealt with by H. J. Eysenck in *The IQ Argument: Race, Intelligence and Education* (1971).

[17] R. R. Walcott, *English Politics in the Early Eighteenth Century* (1956).

[18] A controversy started by R. H. Tawney in 1940. A good review of its progress is contained in the introduction to *Social Change and Revolution in England, 1540–1640,* by Lawrence Stone (1965).

6
Objectives in Society

When attention is directed toward the political, social, and moral activities of man in his societies, we encounter a further step down from the conventional objectivity of scientific research. Just as in the consideration of skills there was encountered a "necessary dependence on the individual," brought about by the inclusion of information relevant to the achievement of the nominated objective but not susceptible of general application, so, in man's social activity, do we meet a further subjectivity produced by the lack of conventionally agreed-upon targets.

By far the greatest part of the discussion of man's social objectives is a discussion of ends which are thought worthy in themselves of achievement. Unlike scientific and skilled activity, in which universal agreement upon a conventionally nominated end serves to harness diverse motives into a pursuit of that end, we are dealing now with objectives which are sought for their own sake. Conventional ends supply external rewards for good performance toward an objective which has low motivating power; real ends have the advantage that the objectives themselves bring direct benefit. No one gains directly from putting a ball into eighteen holes in fewer strokes than others; what one gains are satisfactions contingent upon his excellence in an arbitrary but conventionally recognized objective. He gains self-satisfaction, respect, and perhaps financial reward from what, without society's conventional decision, would be a rather aimless and low-motivating activity. The man whose objective is a larger house, however, can actually enjoy the benefits of the larger house if he achieves that aim. The end itself brings satisfaction sufficient to supply motivation.

It might well be that there are objectives which many people attempt to achieve because they consider them worthy of satisfaction, and it might be that a man who achieves what is generally regarded as a worthy aim can gain the admiration of his peers and a greater degree of self-respect by his achievement. But he still gains the satisfaction of the end itself, and it is still a real aim which people actually wish to achieve, rather than a conventional aim that is pursued for the external gratifications which society has supplied to it. Thus it is quite possible that the man who fulfills his aim of acquiring a larger house might well be looked up to by others as worthy of emulation, and might, in consequence, walk taller himself; but he still gains the tangible benefit he sought, the larger house. Since everyone (by definition) wants to achieve his aims, esteem of a kind is accorded to everyone who fulfills his objectives. He is worthy of admiration as a man who is good at achieving aims, and can be respected in a fashion, regardless of the general opinion concerning the desirability of the ends he pursues. One encounters such remarks as "I do not share his scale of values, but I have to admire the way in which he sets about getting what he wants." But considerably more admiration and esteem are reserved for those who successfully achieve ends which are generally sought after.

Indeed, admiration and esteem are generally regarded as desirable ends. Their pursuit can often involve a person in following ends which he does not regard as worthy in

Trial and Error

themselves but which, because they are generally regarded as worthy, bring with their achievement the externals of praise and respect from other members of society. The individual who seeks fame and admiration can thus be placed in the position of pursuing what, for him, is a purely conventional end but is, for others, an end worthy of achievement in its own right. There is considerable evidence for supposing that many who engage in high-level economic activity do so not for the direct financial gain but for the respect and admiration they believe will accompany a successful performance.[1]

Progress, as mentioned in Chapter 1, must always be aim-related. One does not make progress in the abstract; one makes progress toward the fulfillment of an objective. Now whereas, for activities which have conventionally nominated ends, progress is easy to measure objectively in terms of the end, it is as well to reflect that from the point of view of the participating individuals, progress is made only if achievement of the conventional end in fact brings them closer to achievement of whatever aims led them to undertake the activity. Thus while everyone can speak with confidence of progress in science or in golf, there is not the same confidence in fields which lack conventionally nominated and recognized ends. Real motivation is a personal thing; people have different ideas about which objectives should be pursued and about the comparative rating of objectives which clash with each other. There are reasons for supposing that conscious motives are determined in part by higher ends which are not consciously acknowledged[2] and that people are perhaps more uniform in the pursuit of these higher ends than in accord over their recognized motives; but at the level at which people recognize objectives they think they wish to achieve, there is certainly a wide variety of differing aims.

Progress is the name given to the closer approach to an objective. It can only be used in circumstances in which the objective is admitted and in which a state of attainment is recognized to be nearer that objective than was a previous state. Since real objectives are personal, or applicable only to specified individuals, it follows that progress toward real objectives can only be regarded on a personal level. One man can make progress in any particular field, but one can speak of society as a whole making progress in a field only if it is accepted that either we are using the term *progress* according to the value scale of the individual making the pronouncement or we are talking about circumstances in which society as a whole shares a unifying objective in that field. And since people differ in motives, it is only at the conventional level that we can talk of progress; only at the level where society agrees to *declare* that a particular aim is to be achieved can there be universal estimations of progress. We can speak of progress in science, therefore, not (as Kuhn alleges) because we give the adjective *scientific* to any field in which we recognize progress[3] but because we have accepted a conventional end for scientific activity. The fields in which we cannot agree that there has been progress are those for which we do not have acceptance of a conventional end.

When we say such things as "There has been no progress to speak of in moral thinking," we are not denying the possibility that individuals might have made considerable progress toward their objectives in moral thought. What we are saying is either that there is no aim agreed upon by convention to be the target of moral thinking or that society's attainments in moral thought do not correspond with our own individual ideas.

Progress is made (and recognized as such) by elimination of less adequate attempts to achieve objectives after competitive testing. There is, as we saw, a kind of mental model in the mind of the participant of what the universe should be like after the aim has been achieved. The comparison with that mental model of how the universe actually looks after each attempt affords a basis for appreciating how far short of the

Trial and Error

aim the attempt has fallen. It might suggest ways in which better attempts can be made, and it certainly enables attempts to be evaluated comparatively. In astronomy, a device is occasionally employed which is known as a blink microscope, and which operates on similar principles. To detect nonstellar objects moving against a background of what appears by the earth's rotation to be constant stellar motion, two plates are exposed at some time distance from each other, but showing the same part of the sky. Because the earth's motion is followed by the telescope, the stars appear as points of light in the same position with respect to each other on both plates. Any minor planets, comets, etc., which have an independent motion will appear in different positions on the two plates. In the blink microscope the images are presented to the eyes successively, so that while the stars appear to remain stationary, the objects with independent motion appear to jump back and forth before the eyes, thus enabling the observer to identify them in a large star field. In a way which is similar in many respects, we compare the ideal, imagined state with the actual state after an attempt, and the difference which is revealed between the two is attributed to inadequacies in our attempt. Our competitive testing involves us in continually proposing new alternatives, and discarding whichever produces the greatest divergence between what is intended and what is achieved. Progress comes about because every decision we make is to adopt the better of two alternatives, to adopt the one which produces closer correspondence with the ideal.

When we engage in activities which are delineated by a conventionally nominated objective, we all share the same concept of the ideal; we are all, as it were, using one plate in common when we compare performance attempts. But for activities without an agreed-upon objective, we use different concepts of the ideal; so the approach by one person to his "ideal plate" need not be an approach to the "ideal plate" of another person. It follows from this that any question of "universally recognized progress" does not arise. It is a phrase applicable only to activities which have universally recognized ends.

Even though recognition of progress in the attainment of real objectives might never be universal, there are, of course, fields in which we may say that progress can be *generally* recognized. When the motives are such that they apply to a large proportion of society, that large proportion will be able to talk in terms of general progress toward those ends. This is tantamount to saying that although people have different motives, it might happen that large numbers coincide on particular ones. Since they are using the same notion of the ideal, they will be able to evaluate the performance of others toward that ideal, and to talk of progress being made toward its attainment on something more than an individual basis. This is not to say that progress consists in the nearer approach to what the majority regards as a desirable; it is to say that progress, *for any group,* consists in the nearer approach to what that group regards as a desirable end. Where that group consists of the bulk of a society, one can talk of progress toward general ends, while admitting that they might not be universally sought ends.

The field of economics affords an example. It would be generally accepted, I think, that people seek from economic activity an increasing supply of goods and services. Thus an economic state in which there were more goods and services, and in which they were generally available, would generally be spoken of as representing progress in the economic field. But there might be members of society who regard the prime aim of economic activity as the equalization of the ability to command goods and services, regardless of quantity. If the state of increased goods and services, though these be generally available, and though every member of society be able to command more than before, nonetheless is distributed in such a way that wider disparities exist than before, then the steps that have been taken will be regarded by that minority as a retrogression. Our use of the term *generally recognized progress* thus carries the assumption that there will be some to dispute it, an assumption we do not make when we speak of the recognition as "universal."

When we say such things as "There has been general agreement that our society has made moral progress during the past two hundred years," we do so in the knowledge that the bulk of society would regard it as closer to their ideal if we no longer survey with equanimity the prospect of children under ten being led to a life of hard labor in mines and factories, or human beings being bought and sold for menial servitude. But we do so in full awareness that there are also those in our society who regard such steps as outweighed by what they regard as retrograde steps, such as the preparedness to possess nuclear weapons, and who consequently deny that what has taken place can be called progress.

The difficulties in ascribing progress do not rest with the problem of unshared motives, for there is the added complicating factor that motives change over time. Even if an objective is so widely sought that we can call it a general motive at one stage, we appreciate that it may not always be so in the future. Conventionally nominated objectives rarely change; people might no longer wish to pursue them if they ceased to be accompanied by the external satisfactions of real motive, but the only changes are made to the imposed limitation. We can say that the objective of golf has changed if we introduce a new rule that twenty clubs may be carried; but another (and perhaps more accurate) way of looking at it would be to say that the new objective does not delineate "golf" but some new activity. Certainly, no one could talk sensibly of "changing the objectives of science." What they would mean is that people would be pursuing other objectives than ones which can rightly be called scientific.

Real motives, being unfixed by convention as marking off a particular activity, are subject to change. Whereas the objective of science will always be that of greater predictive power over the observed universe, we cannot say that our economic motives will always be what they are at present. Our real aims, the things we wish to achieve for their own sake, are not selected arbitrarily by ourselves; they are the devices by which we serve more general ends. Thus the man who strives to gain a larger house can, as we saw, actually enjoy the benefits of the larger house if he is successful. But motives such as "desire for larger house" can themselves be generalized under wider headings, such as "desire for personal comfort," and be subject to change if they fail to meet the wider objectives. The man who sought the larger house with a view to promoting his own comfort (and perhaps that of his family) might well find, on inhabiting the new house, that it does not, in fact, make him more comfortable. He might well move out of the larger house in order to serve the requirements of that comfort—rejecting, as it were, his original attempt to make himself more comfortable in favor of a way which his experience has now shown him achieves greater comfort.

It may be appreciated from the example that our aims may change if we find them less adequate than others at achieving the general ends under which they are grouped. Just as we improve our performance toward any end by competitive testing and inadequacy elimination, so can we improve the aims themselves. We reject those whose fulfillment still leaves us dissatisfied in terms of the general end which the initial end was designed to achieve. We can thus see motives as arranged in hierarchical structure, with lesser ones subordinate to higher ones. On each level of the hierarchy there can be progress towards the achievement of superior aims by competitive testing and elimination. There is no reason for any aim to be discarded except that it fails to satisfy us by its fulfillment; and since we must be dissatisfied *in some respect,* we can deduce the operation of a higher aim.

Some of our objectives are undoubtedly unconscious ones.

We find that the achievement of some of our objectives leaves us unsatisfied, without our being able to trace the source of dissatisfaction, and we are left with the expedient of experimenting with different aims to see which of them leave less dissatisfaction by their fulfillment. It is quite possible, therefore, that we can progress to, or regress from, some of our aims without consciously realizing it. It has been proposed, for example, that we have an inborn urge to compete,[4] a genetic drive to fulfill our potential and assert our "identity." If this, or something like it, is indeed an unconscious aim, then we can see how it might come about that the fulfillment of more conscious objectives for security could lead to a blocking of outlets for this unconscious drive, and to consequent feelings of discontent despite the ever-increasing achievement of our recognized aims.[5]

It may well be that there are genetically transmitted unconscious motives of this variety at the apex of the hierarchy of motives. Since motives at each level serve higher motivations, we have to postulate the existence of "highest motivations" in order to avoid the infinite regress. The point can be made that aims that are incompatible with the survival of the species would be selected out by the process of evolutionary elimination; so it would not be unreasonable to propose that the highest motivations would be concerned with evolution and survival, or that they would take the form of inherited instincts. It may be that our unconscious higher motivations are inherited behavioral traits, selected in us by the evolutionary process, and that all our hierarchical motivations are but steps which ascend toward the evolutionary drives of our species.

If all our objectives were but attempts, many stages removed, to fulfill inbuilt drives for "identity," "stimulation," "security,"[6] and the like, it would leave the human race many stages removed from the environmentally determined agents which some thinkers like to propose;[7] but it would still leave considerable scope for the exercise of imagination and critical judgment in devising ways in which higher ends might be served in a way compatible with living in modern societies. Progress toward the achievement of any aims can only be made by competitive testing and inadequacy elimination. And competitive testing requires that competing proposals be formulated. Thus even if man were not in the position of being able to determine the ends which, ultimately, would bring most satisfaction by their fulfillment, he most certainly is in the position of knowing that the degree of satisfaction and fulfillment he achieves is dependent upon his resourcefulness and creative imagination.

Even though man's motives may ultimately have their roots in evolutionary factors, his satisfaction of higher aims is dependent upon his comparative evaluation of proposed secondary aims. It is these aims which change from generation to generation and thus confuse our use of the term *progress*. We are measuring by a shifting scale when we attempt to say that one state of society is better than another. Our very notion of what constitutes "better" may have changed with the transition. Every society sees itself as on a kind of moral plateau; its moral standards are used to evaluate the morality of previous states of society, and even conjectured future states of society. Since its own values form its definition of what is moral, it is inevitable that all behavior that is different from prevailing standards must be regarded as "less moral." The only people who tell us that their own age is less moral than previous ages are those who dissent from their contemporary society's morality and prefer, instead, to adopt the values of the past. Those who adopt the general morality of their contemporary society can only regard previous ages as less moral. Similarly, in the contemplation of future states of society, any standards different from their own are necessarily seen as lower. If they were regarded as higher, society's prevailing morality would have altered. It is much the same as when we attempt to predict what new knowledge will become available in the future. If we can predict it, then we have it already, and it is present and not future knowledge.[8] The only circumstances in which we envisage future society to be more moral are those in which we imagine that more people will adhere in fact to the moral code we now possess in theory. Such circumstances do not represent improved future morality but more widespread obedience to the current moral code; and we are talking about changes in performance, not in objectives.

Evidently it is impossible to talk objectively about progress toward real (as opposed to conventional) ends for two reasons. In the first place, the ends are not universally shared, and in the second place the objectives change over a period of time. We can talk about individuals making progress toward their ends, and we can talk about progress toward general ends when there are objectives which are widely shared by members of a society. Communities *do* have these general ends, even though we allow for the presence of dissenters, because there are factors which militate in favor of the general acceptance of communal objectives and which are, at times, sufficient to overcome the centripetal forces of human variety. Emulation is one such force. Because people have vague and indeterminate aims at the general level, such as desire for comfort, for job satisfaction, for gain, etc., they are able to adopt the more specific aims which are shown by other members of society to be successful at achieving the more general aims. Just as there is "technical knowledge" in the acquisition of a skill, which can be communicated to others and which applies to others, so there are specific aims whose pursuit will, for most people, satisfy general aims. People do not need to make competitive trials at every point; they can emulate the behavior of those who appear to have achieved a desirable degree of success.

Any new idea—be it an aim that is proposed as a way of

satisfying deeper objectives or a proposal of a new attempt to fulfill an existing aim—always starts as the property of the individual who formulates it. If he (and the small circle of those he can influence directly) adopts the innovation and is seen to achieve what others call success, then others will imitate him in its adoption. If this practical test indeed shows increased success for those who follow, they in turn become objects of emulation until the innovation has been widely adopted. By following the lead of the more adventurous members of society, the more cautious members are led into achieving more of their objectives. If the innovation does indeed provide a large proportion of society with increased satisfaction, then we can talk of general progress having been made. Of course, it may come about that either the innovator or some of his emulators achieve results not thought desirable by other members of society—in which case, since it does not serve a general end, the innovation will never become part of generally accepted progress. By emulating success and avoiding failure, society can gain access to tested alternatives and become more uniform in its aims and practices, even though the presence of diverse aims will always mean that some proposals are susceptible of widespread adoption while some are not.

Another factor which helps provide more uniformity is the desire for security in society. There is pressure in society toward the possession of shared values because of the security which accompanies this. The prevalence of shared values reinforces those values; instead of the constant and upsetting questioning of values, there is the knowledge that they are accepted by society and can be held unthinkingly in the forms of custom and tradition. People like, too, to be able to predict what their fellows will do in certain situations; this enables them to plan, with reasonable expectation of success, in their relationships with them and brings the security of feeling adequate to cope with such circumstances as may arise.

To some extent these factors are mutually contradictory.

Desire for shared values cannot always be reconciled with the desire to progress by adopting innovations which have been shown to be successful for others. Despite their apparent incompatibility, society somehow manages to balance these factors against each other, for both may be seen at work, and both contrive to produce rather more "general" values than we might expect in their absence. Both enable us to talk occasionally about progress on a general level rather than an individual one, even though we know that the general level is not universal.

The implication of our discussion of true motives has been that progress toward their attainment, like progress toward the nominated end of science, is founded upon *creative* acts. And as, in science, we are wrong to think in terms of a "correct explanation" waiting to be discovered by us, so, in the achievement of our true objectives, are we wrong to think in terms of a "correct" way of doing things. In science we propose models creatively, and retain those which serve our purpose better than it was served before. So, in the achievement of our nonconventional aims, do we creatively devise new attempts (in the form of actions or subordinate aims) to achieve our purposes better than did our previous creations. Progress in our nonconventional ends means that we have devised proposals which, after critical testing, we prefer over our previously adopted proposals as better serving our purposes. If those purposes be diverse among people, then so must be the adopted proposals which will represent progress. When we talk of "generally" accepted progress, therefore, we are doing no more than using a term of convenience which we are enabled to use because the motives of men happen to coincide. Progress that is generally recognized as such is not "greater" or somehow "better" progress than that which lacks this recognition. It is simply progress which is more evident because it represents the nearer achievement of a widely held objective.

We have no grounds from the foregoing argument to suppose that humanity makes more progress by agreeing on what are the true motivations of man. The agreement to declare a conventional objective will produce a situation in which we are more likely to progress toward that objective; but we cannot assume that the pathway to progress in our moral and political life will begin with the recognition of identical aims among men. If, for any objective, there comes the discovery and admission that it *is* a universal end of man,[9] then society will be able to agree that the progress made toward that end can be described as progress for society. But this public recognition of progress does not make it any more or less real. *Progress* refers to the nearer approach to objectives, whether or not this is recognized and widely admitted. The discovery and recognition of universal ends simply means that everyone may now apply the term *progress* where only some used it before.

Because true motivations are individual, so must be the idea of progress toward their fulfillment. If it happens that everyone discovers they coincide in their views on the desirability of any particular objective, it will happen that, in this respect at least, their opinions of what constitutes progress will coincide. But it is their opinion we are talking about, their estimation—rather than the fact. If the members of a society pursue aims on which they are not agreed, it might come about that all of them could approach nearer to achieving those aims, and all could be said to make progress, even though they themselves would not agree on that. We cannot assume that in a situation where some members of society regard an aim as desirable, while others do not, that one group is necessarily "right" and the other "wrong." It might be that all of them were pursuing (perhaps unconsciously) a higher aim, and that the secondary aim was held in the manner of a conjecture as to what might achieve the higher aim. In such a case, critical testing would tell whether the achievement of the secondary aim served the higher aim better than nothing at all, or better

Trial and Error

than any proposed alternatives. But there might be alternatives, not yet proposed, which would serve the higher aim better. Thus even if it could be shown that adoption of the secondary aim *did* serve the higher aim, it might also be shown, subsequent to that demonstration, that nonadoption served the higher aim better. It would seem "right" at one time and "wrong" at another.

Our recognition that progress starts with the creative act of a new conjecture is important. Just as it is incorrect to think of science as the gaining of increasing access to a body of objective truth by eliminating what is not true, it is equally incorrect to think of moral and political progress in terms of the systematic elimination of "wrong" alternatives. The mental conception of progress should be one of systematic building, rather than whittling away. It is not the case that in the pursuit of our true aims we attempt to discover the best way of achieving them by the gradual abandonment of ways which are not the best. It *is* the case that our achievement depends upon our ability to *create* ways which are better than the ones we created before, as well as on our ability to establish which way is better by competitive testing.

Followers of John Stuart Mill would have it that, in such activities as the pursuit of our aims, no one can ever be certain that he is right. They advocate political liberty on the grounds that we can never know that a proposal is wrong, and cannot, therefore, be justified in forbidding it.[10] The point is that we cannot even assume there is such a thing as "right" in this sphere. It is not so much that we can never recognize it for certain as that it does not exist at all. We are dealing with creations of the human mind that can be compared, in practice, to see if they are "better" or "worse" than each other at achieving what they were devised to achieve. We know, too, that since the motives vary with individuals, so will the comparisons of the success of proposals. What is "better" for one might not be so for another. There is little to be gained by the suggestion that "ultimately, we all seek the same thing." As indicated, it might well be that, at the level of "highest motivations," we all indeed share common evolutionary ends. But it is undoubtedly true that some, if not all, of these "highest motivations" are ones we pursue unconsciously, and which lie beyond the range of our introspection. We are dependent for their fulfillment on our more conscious, secondary aims. And the decision as to which secondary aims will best serve these higher ends can only be made on the basis of competitive testing. It cannot be deduced, only proposed and tested.

Notes

[1] In the upper echelons of the world of business, high salaries are apparently regarded more as marks of status than direct measures of spending power. With high marginal rates of taxation, the difference between £45,000 and £55,000 is very small in terms of what it will buy; to the status-conscious director, however, it can be vital. When Dr. Beeching left I.C.I. to become the director of British Rail, he insisted on not accepting a salary lower than the £24,000 he was already being paid—so that, he explained publicly, the move would not be regarded as a demotion.

[2] This is the point dealt with in chapter 2 and amplified in footnote 16 of that chapter.

[3] Thomas S. Kuhn, *The Structure of Scientific Revolutions* (1962).

[4] Suggested by Robert Ardrey in *The Territorial Imperative* (1966), ch. 5, and amplified in his *Social Contract* (1970), ch. 3.

[5] One of Ardrey's points (in *The Social Contract*) is that one explanation of juvenile violence in our societies is that life has been made "too safe." By denying opportunities to respond to challenge and danger, we have (claims Ardrey) produced a situation in which our youth feels the need to "prove" itself on the streets in acts of vandalism and gang violence.

[6] These are the three "basic drives" which Ardrey proposes in the works cited.

[7] This is an allusion to the school of environmental sociology which has B. F. Skinner (*Science and Human Behavior* [1953] and *The Phylogeny and Ontogeny of Behaviour* [1966]) as one of its high priests.

[8] Popper uses this idea as an outline refutation of historicism in his *Poverty of Historicism* (first published 1944/45, in book form 1957). Because the course of human history is influenced by the growth of knowledge, we can therefore reject the possibility of a *theoretical history* (preface of the 1957 edition, op. cit.). My point on morality is that we cannot now admit the superiority of tomorrow's values (even if we could know them), for to admit that would be to adopt those values in preference to our present ones.

[9] The recognition of a common aim *actually possessed* is not to be equated with general concurrence in a decision to *make* something a common aim by convention.

[10] F. A. von Hayek (*The Constitution of Liberty* [1960]) has been the principal exponent of this view.

7
Progress in Economic Life

In activities which are not delineated by the acceptance of a conventionally nominated end, then, we are faced by a hierarchy of real and imagined aims which varies from individual to individual, even though it is possible that people share common evolutionary goals at the apex of the hierarchy.[1] Despite numerous attempts, no reductionist school has ever managed to establish that human motivations can be derived from one basic, common aim. All have it in common that, because actual behavior does not lend itself readily to such a unification, many of our apparent aspirations must be stretched on the rack or have their head and feet lopped off in order that they might fit onto the single-model bed.

The weaknesses of these proposed reductions have been widely exposed, and although some workers who are active in the social sciences still attempt to bring human aims down to basic drives, the relative force of these drives, and hence their priority in the hierarchy, is admitted to vary with the individual. The only unification ever to gain wide acceptance in a society was the hedonistic utilitarianism of Bentham in nineteenth-century Britain. Bentham's contentions, that whatever it is we think we seek, we seek it for the favorable balance of pleasure over pain which is consequent upon it, and that this quantification can be summed from the individual to the society, were popularized into the catchphrase "the greatest happiness of the greatest number," and caught the ear of those in power.

Following from the discussion of progress and conventional ends, we may note that it was during the period of British history when this doctrine was paramount that there was the most widespread belief in moral progress.[2] With the influence of men such as Bentham and Chadwick, the utilitarian thesis had considerable influence on legislation, and was so widely accepted that it assumed (temporarily) something approaching the status of a conventional end of the leaders of society. This was the period which saw factory acts and mines acts, laws limiting the working hours for women and children, the abolition of slavery, and the rise of an inspectorate and a civil service. It was a period during which a large proportion of those in power was convinced that progress was being made. They thought, too, that they had a standard, independent of personal opinion, against which that progress could be measured. Although hedonistic utilitarianism cannot now be regarded as the basis of all value and motivation, few would dispute that the nineteenth-century legislators did indeed bring greater happiness to greater numbers, and did indeed approach nearer what they regarded as the fundamental objective.[3]

The question we now propose to consider is whether there can be any general assessment or awareness of progress in the absence of any kind of objective standard. Can there be, in other words, any idea of progress when we deal with activities in which the ends are not conventionally nominated? In the first instance, the answer must be that there cannot. If there is no agreed-upon end, people cannot estimate performance in terms of an ideal and cannot, therefore, talk of progress toward it. But there is a sense in which the members of a society can be agreed that there has been progress, even where they are not in agreement over the ends to be pursued. It is possible that in some activities people can pursue different aims, and yet all can make progress simultaneously toward the achievement of those individual aims. Although the term *progress* is normally used in an aim-related way, as "progress toward something," we can readily conceive of situations in which it could be used *without the aim being specified.* A teacher at a craft school may say, "All the pupils made good progress," without necessarily implying that all were attempting to achieve the same thing. Some might have studied needlework, some basketry, some cooking, and some weaving; but if all approached nearer to proficiency in whatever aims they had set for themselves, it would be sensible to speak collectively of the whole class as making progress.

Progress is here taken to mean "advancement toward the aim, *whatever it might be.*" If asked in what field the progress had been made, the teacher could only reply by enumerating the individual aims of the members of the class or by giving a general answer such as "handicrafts," which conceals the disparate aims included under this heading. The situation described by the example is a limited one. We are talking here of progress in fields which permit a variety of individual motives to fall under their terms of reference, and we are talking about motives which refer to the desired achievement of the individual who holds them, rather than a desire for *others* to behave in a particular way.

Obviously, if the motives are of a type which require suitable behavior on the part of others before they can be fulfilled, then we meet with a possible conflict of motives. The person who is required to behave in a particular way to fulfill another's motive might find that this required behavior does not enable him to achieve his own aims. Only in a situation where the motives refer exclusively to those motivated can such conflict be eliminated. In the handicraft class of our example, it is assumed that each person's aim is proficiency for himself in his chosen craft. Because his aim does not involve others in the achievement of ends which he nominates, his progress does not interfere with theirs. The other members of the class pursue their individual aims in a similar fashion. Because the progress of some does not involve the retardation or retrogression of others, we can speak of the class as a whole as making progress.

This is a very different case from one we considered before,[4] in which we talked of two people with contradictory motives and envisaged a situation in which a new state would mean progress toward his aim for one but (necessarily) regression for the other. The point of difference in our new example is that we are talking neither about conflicting aims nor about states of achievement common to the holders of different aims. In the handicraft class, any new "state" is a state of achievement in which only one individual finds himself: we are talking about a situation in which actions are individual rather than collective. We say that the whole class made progress if each of its individual states of achievement represents an advance toward individual aims from the previous state. We are summing elements which do not mix. Just as there is no composite sum of "my shoes plus your spectacles," there is no sum of several different states of performance in different activities by different people. But we can certainly talk about an increase in the composite if every single element is larger. Thus if my shoes are replaced by a larger pair and your spectacles are replaced by a larger pair, we know that the new "my shoes plus your spectacles" is larger than before. What we cannot do is give comparative weighting to the individual items; we cannot say that an increase in size of spectacles makes up for a decrease in size of shoes.

The analogy is helpful because it may be seen that if two people, pursuing nonconflicting aims, both make progress, we can talk of the two *collectively* making progress; whereas if one advances and one regresses, we have no common scale on which to determine whether one's advance compensates for the other's regression. We talk of progress in general terms, too, where a large number of people are engaged in activities grouped under a general heading, and where a great majority of them make individual progress. While we cannot assume that the progress of one can compensate for the regression of another, we tend to assume, with very large numbers, that progress for most of them enables us to talk about "the progress of the group" or "collective progress." While we have no system of calculus which enables us to weight the progress of some against the regression of others, we assume that the regression of a very small subgroup is outweighed by the advancement of a large majority. Utilitarian theory, although faced by a similar problem in being unable to weight the pleasure of some against the pain of others, nonetheless advocated the taking of decisions in which a "slight" unhappiness of a few was accompanied by a greatly increased happiness of many. While it might be difficult to decide whether the unhappiness of one, however slight, could be counterbalanced by the happiness of two, it was recognized as easier to make the decision where the happiness of two thousand lay on the other side.[5] Similarly, while a class of three members might not lead us to talk in terms of "collective progress" if two had advanced and one had regressed, we would use the term without much hesitation if it were a case of two thousand nearing their aims and only one receding.

It comes about, therefore, that the term *progress* is used in the case of large numbers of people, pursuing disparate aims under a general heading, where a large majority of them take steps which bring them closer to achievement of their individual aims. But only for activities in which the individual aims relate only to the performance of the motivated person can the conflict of ends be avoided. In cases where the fulfillment of an aim will require appropriate behavior by those not sharing the aim, it will be impossible to talk of progress by a group generally, but only of progress from the point of view of certain members of the group.

Economic activity is a field in which disparate aims may be followed by participating individuals, and in which it may sometimes happen that the vast majority, by making advances toward their individually different ends, will enable us to talk of the "economic progress" of a society. It may be possible to talk of the collective economic aims of a society if it happens that a very large majority opinion is anxious for its society to achieve common ends in the economic sphere. But whether or not a society has any collective economic ends, it is certainly true that the individuals within it have personal economic aims. The economic objective varies from individual to individual; it might be more consumer goods, greater security, more leisure time, or any combination which allows unequal weight to one aspect, depending upon the circumstances and the character of the person concerned. These objectives are all of the self-referring type, which deal with the state of achievement of the individual himself; but ideological aims are expressed in the economic sphere which refer to the achievement of others. If one person has for his aim that all people will own an equal quantity of goods, then this is evidently not a self-referring aim, and it is, moreover, one which we can expect to conflict with individual self-referring aims. It will not be possible for that person to fulfill his aim at the same time as others satisfy their different desires for quantities of goods.

Because economic aims of the self-referring variety tend to be comparatives, it is possible for people to move simultaneously toward their achievement. The aim to acquire a particular house must inevitably clash with the identical aim of someone else; but the aim for a larger house can be satisfied for several people simultaneously. When it was thought that total wealth was fixed,[6] it was also thought that comparative aims were conflicting. Thus if one person is to acquire more

Trial and Error

from a fixed supply, others must receive less. The only way in which a whole society could advance simultaneously was thought to be at the expense of other societies. In modern industrial economies, though, it is easier to appreciate that wealth is continually created, that it is possible for comparative advance to be made without disadvantage to anyone. There are modern economies in which all members of society can (in theory) approach nearer a variety of economic aims without necessarily thwarting others from doing likewise. Of course, this applies only to self-referring economic ends; it is not possible for people to advance simultaneously toward what they want to do and also toward what someone else wants them to do, except in the remarkable case of coincidence.

We can easily conceive of states of society in which we can say that there is economic progress because all the individuals within them have advanced further toward their variety of ends. We can also conceive of societies in which the ends are determined centrally by those in power, and in which there can be progress toward those ends. Only in the first type of society, though, will there be none to contradict the use of the term.

When we look at the way in which people attempt to achieve their economic objectives, we can see how the method which has already been inspected comes to be applied. Provided people keep clear sight of their objectives, they are able to improve their performance by elimination of inferior alternatives after comparative testing. Many of what we refer to as "market mechanisms" are really no more than the summation of many attempts by many people to achieve their economic aims. Consider, for example, the man selling goods. For a fixed supply, he knows when the price is too high because his goods remain unsold; when it is too low, he is unable to meet the demand. Because his aim is to sell all the goods at the best possible price, he will reject as inferior those attempts to establish the price which will leave him with unsold goods, or those which leave him without goods to sell. His "equilibrium price" is the price at which he can "just" sell all his goods. The equilibrium price in economics represents that process magnified many times. Because sellers generally wish to sell all their goods at the best possible price, and because buyers wish to pay as little as is necessary to secure the article, a price is arrived at where the supply coincides with the demand. The converging adjustments made by individuals in response to their first attempts (and the consequences which follow) are writ large on the economic situation. Because an assumed aim of the buyer is to make his resources stretch to the maximum quantity of goods, he will buy where it is cheapest to do so. The effect of this aim, multiplied by thousands, is to make prices roughly equal: if one seller undercuts, he will corner the market; so the others must follow suit or be left with unsold goods.[7]

The aims of buyer and seller are contradictory. The seller wants to sell dearly; the buyer to buy cheaply. The market mechanism of the equilibrium price is a kind of compromise. It represents the most that each of them can fulfill of his own aims without prejudice to the aims of the other. Both aims are derivative from higher aims: the seller wants to sell dearly in order to make more money, or in order to satisfy his needs with minimum work; the buyer wants to stretch his resources in order to maximize his quantity of goods, or to enjoy more leisure time. It is quite possible that the seller would accept a lower price if he could sell more (thus making more money), or that the buyer would pay a higher price if he could save time by doing so. All of these motives are found at work in any economic situation. The corner shop, for example, remains in business, despite its higher prices, because *convenience* is included among economic ends.

These market mechanisms are not devices which have been invented in order to accommodate conflicting motives; they are a direct reflection of the operation of individual motives, in a sense the sum of them. Increased supply in times of scarcity is an effect produced by the economic aims of individuals. When goods are scarce the seller has an advantage, and is able to charge a higher price because people will bid against each other to acquire the scarce goods (or services). But the higher prices cause more resources to be committed as other people attempt to maximize their gains by taking advantage of the newly increased profitability; and the increase in supply naturally lowers the price as people no longer need to outbid each other to the same extent.[8] Similarly, in a glut situation, prices tend to fall (as sellers strive to dispose of surplus goods and services by undercutting each other), and fewer resources are committed because the fall in price means there is more profit to be made elsewhere.

Economic man, like scientific man, is concerned with imaginative proposing and with testing. Scientific man wants to extend his predictive power; he seeks proposed models with "surplus corroborated empirical content," the ones which pass the test of prediction. Economic man seeks such things as maximization of profit, purchase of goods and services at the cheapest price, greatest return on investment, etc. When economic man makes his proposal, be it what to produce, what process to employ, where to invest, what price to charge, then he has some idea of what he wants to achieve. Often his aim will be a simple comparative (or a superlative): if he seeks return on capital, he will attempt to obtain the *greatest* return; if he is after profit, he will seek *more* profit. But it is not always so. He might simply seek a comfortable living, an involvement in the economic system which leaves him some free time to himself. There is reason to suppose that many participants in economic activity seek the lack of worry which accompanies a steady and secure job, combined with the reasonable expectancy of a systematic and unidirectional advance in purchasing power. The point is that the participant has to test proposed alternatives, and judge them on the basis of the results achieved. If the return on investment falls short of the aim, he can try somewhere else with his capital, and reject the inferior attempt. If he cannot sell enough of his goods, he can change the price or change the product. Always it is the result after testing which he compares with his aims in order to see how far short of successful was his proposal.

It is of course true that economic situations become exceedingly complex, and that such decisions may involve consideration of many factors. But the principles remain the same: the proposal is followed by the practical test, which is followed in turn by modification of performance in order to approach more nearly the desired end. Faced by the fact that he is unable to supply a demand, the seller has to consider such factors as whether a price rise on his part would bring more competition into the field to take advantage of the increased profits; for a wrong guess on his part would do just that. Even finer judgments are required from the producer when he has to decide whether to produce more goods in response to an excess of demand, and if so, how much more.

As with scientific discovery, it is not only the proposer who learns. In economic activity the results of his tests are available for inspection by others (in most aspects), who may take the lessons about what to do or what to avoid. This facet is important for a market economy because, since it deals with economic situations in which no single producer, supplier, or consumer can noticeably affect the equilibrium by his individual activities, emulation helps ensure that successful proposals have their effects on a prevailing situation.

In science there is a conventional target of increased predictive power, a target by whose achievement the fulfillment of real aims can be brought about. The scientist may be motivated by desire for wealth or glory, but it is increased predictive power he must aim at in order to secure them. While the targets are not conventional in the economic sphere, the type of economic organization of a society determines what must be achieved if real aims are to be satisfied. In a market economy the ultimate test is whether the proposals involve the production or provision of goods and services which people will be prepared to buy, and at a price they are prepared to pay. This is not something which has at any stage been agreed upon as a worthy target: it is not conventional in that sense. But in an economy that is characterized by the voluntary exchange of money for goods and services, resources are accumulated by supplying a product or service which people prefer to possess, rather than resources they already possess. The test of the proposal is whether the product or service sells. It is the consumer, at the end of the chain, who either makes the decision to buy or commits his limited resources elsewhere. In a competitive situation (of the market economy), retailers compete with each other to sell to consumers, wholesalers compete with each other to sell to retailers, and producers compete with each other to sell to wholesalers. If the consumer will not buy the product, then the retailer will not buy it from the wholesaler, nor the wholesaler from the manufacturer; and the manufacturer will have to stop producing it. In such a situation, it is only by having consumers sufficiently satisfied to buy that the retailer, wholesaler, and producer can hope to achieve their objectives.

There is thus in a market economy an objective whose achievement is required if the real aims of the participants are to be fulfilled. It is an objective that is independent of the private motives of individuals, whose relation to it is only that their satisfaction is dependent upon the degree to which they serve it successfully. There may be those engaged in economic activity who hold the real aim of bringing satisfaction to others, just as there may be scientific workers genuinely anxious to extend predictive power; but in each case the appropriate objective must be pursued, whether or not it is a real aim, in order that people might gain success in whatever they are attempting to achieve.

The fact that the consumer's readiness to buy represents

the vital test means that, in a competitive market situation,[9] production and distribution will tend to converge toward consumer satisfaction. In science the process converges on ever-increasing ability to predict the observed universe, because this target constitutes the vital test, and because attempts are rejected if they are shown to be inferior to others at achieving that target. Similarly in the economic sphere, because the preparedness of the consumer to part with his resources constitutes the vital key to success, proposals are rejected which are found to be inferior in that respect. Thus we can say that the system produces a convergence toward increasing consumer satisfaction.

The point may be illustrated by consideration of the entry into a prevailing market situation of a competitor who can produce more cheaply than existing producers, either by reason of more efficient organization or by virtue of a technological advance. The newcomer will be able to sell more cheaply than his competitors. Because people wish to buy as cheaply as possible (with quality considered constant), he will capture a large share of the market. He will make more profit, and will thus have more resources to commit to production, and will be able to expand. Not only this, but because he is more profitable he will find it easier to attract investment from outside, since investors seek high returns on capital. Other producers, on the reverse side of the coin, will find they are selling less. The effect of the newcomer's production coming onto the market will be to lower prices to the level at which it is not worth their while (but still worth his while) continuing to produce. They (or others) may copy the successful innovation of the newcomer and become able to produce more cheaply themselves. The effect is a tendency toward the cheapest method of production, and this effect is brought about because the consumers wish to buy as cheaply as possible.

Again, we might consider the activity of the entrepreneur. He has thought of a refinement or an improvement, or a new product or service, he thinks the public will wish to buy. When the critical test comes, and if the consumers buy his product in preference to others, then his competitors will be forced to follow his lead, to accept a serious decline in their business, or to attempt innovations of their own. If he fails the test, on the other hand, and consumers do not wish to buy his product, he will go out of business, perhaps losing all the money he invested in the experiment. The activities of the entrepreneur provide a particularly dramatic form of elimination by competitive testing, since his fate is usually tied to that of his proposal. If the proposal is superior to its alternatives, he personally will make money; if it is inferior, he will fail with it. The market allows him to take tremendous risks, but it allows him tremendous rewards for success. And "success" consists in the production of goods and services the public prefers to buy. The effect of the accumulated testing and elimination activities of entrepreneurs is thus to produce more and better goods the public wants, and in ways which are increasingly efficient. The more entrepreneurs there are, the more dynamic will be the economy, and the more dramatic will be its performance at producing more and better and cheaper goods.

The heady whirl of business enterprise might seem to be far removed from the activity of the scientist, who sits dispassionately making observations to check against his theories, but both businessman and scientist are engaged in a similar process. The scientist is aiding the progress of predictive power by enabling new and better models to supplant the old, while the businessman is aiding the progress of consumer satisfaction by enabling new and better products and processes to supplant the old. Each makes his proposal, and each performs his experiment. Each may find that the results of that experiment make him reject his proposal, and each may modify the original attempt in the light of those results. Or each may discover that the test results enable him to prefer the new proposal over its predecessors. The scientist may find some day that a new experiment means his model must be supplanted, just as the successful businessman may one day be forced out of business by a better innovation. Both are engaged in the pursuit of an end whose fulfillment is increasingly required if their own aims are to be achieved. Both are involved in the quest for progress.

A system which converges toward consumer satisfaction has space within it for the satisfaction of many economic ends. Not only can the public obtain the quantity and variety of goods it seeks, but there is scope for the pursuit of ends not directly related to material goods. If the effect of testing and elimination is to produce more, better, and cheaper goods, then a person will be able to command a sufficiency on smaller resources. This gives him the option of purchasing more goods or preferring to take more leisure time.

While many regard increased material affluence as "progress" because it advances them toward their aims, there are undoubtedly others who rate nonmaterial satisfactions more highly, and whose aims can be satisfied more by increased time with their family or friends, or in the pursuit of private hobbies or interests. It is thus possible that a market economy, by converging toward increasing consumer satisfaction, could lead to increased fulfillment of a variety of private objectives. It could (and does) produce situations in which a society can be said to make economic progress because individuals within that society are able to approach nearer the achievement of disparate aims. It is quite possible that we could describe a general increase in prosperity as "progress" for a society because it enabled the members of that society to pursue their own ends more effectively. Prosperity brings power in its wake: men have to commit less time to attaining self-sufficiency, and fewer resources to achieving security. Whether the surplus time is used to achieve greater wealth or greater independence from the productive process depends upon the private motivations of the individual concerned.

Trial and Error

The consideration of economics on which these arguments have been raised has been devoted to only a few theoretical elements of a market economy situation. It might well be argued that when attention is turned to practical aspects, to the consideration of actual economies, such things as free competition and the absence of monopoly power are nowhere to be realized. Real economies are characterized by such factors as *laissez faire,* which allows the build-up of coercive power by big suppliers of capital, goods, or labor,[10] and by *central direction,* which substitutes political control for consumer preference as the driving force of the system. Such factors, where they are permitted or implemented, do indeed limit the capacity possessed by the theoretical market model to allow scope for the fulfillment of private ends. They represent the imposition of ends upon the economic system. Monopoly and the coercive power of capital or labor represent an attempt to achieve independence from the instability of a changing market, while central direction represents the attempt to make the economy achieve either the objectives of the rulers or what they think are the collective ends of society.

The theoretical market model we considered was one in which consumer preference was the ultimate test by which proposals were retained, rejected, or modified. It is easy to see why people, in their capacity as consumers, should prefer a system which converges toward satisfying their preferences, toward production of more and better and cheaper goods, and which allows space within it for the increasing attainment of nonmaterial, as well as material, objectives. This is no reason why people, acting in other economic capacities, should prefer such a system. It might be efficient, but it is also risky, and at times costly, to those who make unsuccessful proposals. People tend to prefer a state of affairs in which they have more stability in their individual situation; they prefer, in other words, to remove the element of fortune.

Why should a producer be exposed to the vagaries of the

price mechanism if he can capture a sufficient share of the market to be independent of it? Why should he risk being driven out of business by more efficient competitors if he can buy them out? Why should he take the chance of the public's not wanting his product if he can make them buy it by "coercive" advertising?[11] Why should a man let the price of his labor be dependent upon the preparedness of an unpredictable public to buy the product he makes, when he can, by combining, use collective power to assert a price for it?[12] All of these questions show how a drive for security of position can easily subvert the principles of the market economy. They illustrate a basic truth about human nature: no one likes a price ring when he is buying, but everyone likes one when he is selling.[13] They represent the attempt to gain the benefit of progress, brought about by the testing and inadequacy elimination of others, while rendering oneself invulnerable to the inevitable changes which are consequent upon it.

Progress necessarily involves change, change from a previous state of performance to a new state which is closer to the conception of the ideal that is sought. Change might be valuable in bringing people nearer to objectives, but it is a source of worry and upset to those affected directly by it. Any society which was committed to economic "progress," to the provision of more and better and cheaper goods, would have to accept the consequences of change which were necessary for its accomplishment. A mobile labor force, ever ready to learn new skills and to change jobs, is an inevitable consequence of the elimination of less adequate economic proposals and practices. A changing flow of successful businesses is another such consequence. No society which refused to accept such consequences could hope to engage in the rapid turnover of proposals and tests which is part of the method of making progress.

The centrally directed economy is not necessarily immune from the climate of change which characterizes the market

Trial and Error

model, for it is itself a system designed to achieve objectives. Although the objectives are predetermined by the controllers, instead of being the private aims of those participating, the economy is still subject to trial and inadequacy elimination as the attempt is made to bring its performance into line with the ideal. Obviously, a centrally directed economy can be geared to the achievement of arbitrary ends, such as, for example, a 200 percent increase in steel production, by making those ends the ideal against which actual performance is measured when proposals are compared. Those directives which do not bring about the required increase in steel production can be rejected in favor of those which do. If proposals are judged against the standard of what is required, then each decision will be to prefer an attempt which succeeds more than its rivals at achieving what is required. When simple, limited aims are being considered, the controlled system can undoubtedly bring about progress toward them. It will be thought of as "progress" only by those who hold those aims, since the average citizen of such an economy will hardly describe an increase in steel production as progress if its achievement involves the negation of his private objectives. The progress of directed economies is limited to a convergence on the aims actually nominated; there may be all kinds of side consequences which follow from the achievement of nominated ends, and which are unacceptable by the standard of undeclared aims.

It is claimed of centrally directed economies that they enable the real aims of members of society to be fulfilled more adequately than do market economies. The contention is that not only are they more effective in the pursuit of arbitrary ends nominated by the controllers, but they are better at achieving the production of more and better and cheaper goods, with the consequent increase in the ability of the citizen to fulfill his private objectives. The market economy, it is pointed out, is *wasteful*. Many of its participants are engaged in the inefficient production of the "wrong" sort of goods, waiting for consumer preference to deliver a verdict on their activities which will ultimately count them out of the economic process. In arguments which have certainly found the ear of government, it has been pointed out that a market situation takes time to sort out the efficient from the inefficient, the wanted product from the unwanted.

If, instead of relying on the haphazard operations of testing and inadequacy elimination, an overall plan were made for a fixed period of economic progress (five years seems to be a favorite), it is claimed that the priorities could be sorted out in advance, the most efficient production methods could be used by all, and the resources could be allocated over the whole economy in an interlocking way. The advantages would be that no production would be wasted in the blind alleys of methods which a market situation would have taken time to weed out; that raw materials, which take time to prepare, could be got ready in advance; and that the required quantity of production could be known accurately and achieved accordingly.

This planned economy is also capable of improvement by testing and elimination. The "five-year plan" is the proposal, and its results in practice can be compared with the desired objectives to see how good was the proposal, and how the next one might be improved. But the "priorities" to be "sorted out in advance" are the objectives that are nominated by the controllers as the important ones; they are not necessarily the priorities of the participants. Even if the planners attempt to assess the real motives of the members of society, there is no assurance that they will be correct in their assessment, or even that there will be sufficient unanimity for general assessments to be made at all. The proposed use of "the most efficient production methods" implies that they are either known or can in some way be computed. Our previous argument carried the implication that these methods were discovered by testing competing proposals. If one is selected for overall application,

Trial and Error

there is not only the possibility that it will not be the most efficient but there will be no means of ascertaining this fact in the absence of competitors. The allocation of resources in such a way that no production would be "wasted" means, in effect, that only one proposal is tested in each field.

The "wastage" of the market economy is like the "wastage" of less adequate scientific models. It would be much more efficient, it seems, if scientists did not waste time on theories which were later rejected but spent their efforts, instead, on ones which could be preferred. The point is, of course, that only comparative testing tells us which ones *are* to be preferred; it is absurd to suggest that we should confine our attentions to good models, when the standard of "good" relates to their superiority over the "bad" ones, a superiority that is revealed only by spending time on both. The "wastage" of a market economy represents the discovery of superior ways; rejected ways are wastage only because better ways are found by comparative testing. Without testing, we have no reason to prefer one proposal to another. The elimination of "wastage" is the elimination of that comparison which is so essential for progress.

Finally, it may be said of the "planned" economic model that it is by no means obvious that the "required" quantity of production can be "known accurately," even if the nominated figure could indeed be "achieved accordingly." If a target is to be set for planned achievement, that target must be as accurate a prediction as possible of what will be needed. Is it to be the planners' view of what people will need, or an attempted estimate of what people themselves think they will need? In the first case, there is no reason to suppose that the valuation of the planners is superior to that of the people, and in the second case there is no reason to suppose that such calculations will be correct. To estimate, years in advance, what goods people will need, in what quantities, varieties, styles, and colors, is difficult enough, even without taking account of changing circumstances and fashions, let alone scientific and technological advances.[14]

It is a serious weakness of the centrally directed economy that there can be little basis for assessment of performance. The planners can compare the achievement with the ideal, and modify accordingly; but they have no comparative selection of proposals to make, since only one was tried. If a prediction is made concerning which products, which varieties, and in which quantities people will wish to buy, and if they are then produced successfully according to the plan, people will have to accept them in the absence of alternatives. A five-year plan can predict what numbers, styles, and colors of shoes people will want; and people will have no option, if they need shoes, but to buy what is produced. Since all the shoes are bought, the planners can congratulate themselves on a "successful" prediction, without having an opportunity to learn from their mistakes. In a market situation, producers who predicted inaccurately would suffer economic consequences, while successful guessers would enjoy rewards and find resources allocated their way for further production of what was required. In the absence of alternatives, any situation can be shown to be "adequate," and there is no stimulus toward progress.

Thus even where the objectives of the planned economy are confined to those nominated by the planners, progress can only be made toward these aims in discrete stages; the performance of the proposal at one time can only be rated against the performance of another proposal at another time. In a market situation, on the other hand, the multiplicity of proposals under test means that there is continual progress toward the aims of the participating individuals. Where the aim of the planned economy is to achieve the wider objectives of the members of society by aiming at such targets as the production of more and better and cheaper goods, the absence of competitive testing makes the disparity even more apparent.

Trial and Error

The economic plan is a conjunction of many proposals, which range over various aspects of the economy. An inadequate result (even where there is the basis for appreciating which results *are* inadequate) will not necessarily reveal the source of the inadequacy. Because so many aspects are tested together, it is more difficult to know where to apply modification proposals. In a market economy, less adequate proposals are continually replaced at the source by more adequate proposals: because the testing is performed individually in discrete sections of the economy, each section can benefit from elimination of inferior alternatives. The result of the inferior alternative can be inspected when and where it happens, and can serve as a basis for immediate decision. When one conjoined proposal is made over an extended period, deficient aspects are not so readily identified.

One factor which serves to assist progress is awareness of what is possible. We saw in the section on skills how attainment levels come to be set, dependent to some extent on the conception of possible levels. It was noted that an awareness of new possibilities can raise both the target and the achieved level. It is an obvious weakness of the centrally directed economy that awareness of new possibilities is inhibited by the achievement of preconceived performance levels. If, from our previous examples, all of the produced shoes were actually bought, then neither planners nor public might have any idea of what *could* have been achieved, except perhaps by external comparison with the attainments of market economies elsewhere. The market situation, by allowing those with successful proposals to achieve more than others, inculcates not only emulation of the proposals but emulation of the objectives. It serves to bring about awareness of what others can do, and so raises the economic sights of everyone. The directed system not only precludes emulation of independently tested proposals, it also prevents the example of visible higher targets.

In either system a proposal might involve unexpected and unacceptable side consequences, consequences discoverable only by testing. In a market situation, where different competing proposals are tested, one such unfortunate instance does not drag down the whole economy, it merely removes those who implemented it. A few people go out of business or, if they are lucky, escape by merely abandoning the proposal. A bad guess of this nature in a planned economy might mean that resources were committed on a large scale to production methods which involved unacceptable consequences. In the monolithic economies, the eggs are entrusted to one basket, and all may break if the basket falls. The pluralistic economy achieves a kind of safety in its variety: the unacceptable can be removed as part of a continuous process of testing before its mistakes are repeated on the large scale.

There is not only safety in variety but an increased probability of successful proposals. As we saw in science, the more creative minds that are at work formulating and testing new proposals, the greater chance that some will be found to be superior to existing ones. When the United States government committed itself in the Second World War to the manufacture of an atomic bomb, it set about the task by proceeding with several alternative solutions simultaneously, estimating (correctly) that the discovery of a workable one would thereby be accelerated. The process of gaseous diffusion emerged as the preferable solution during development of the Manhattan Project. In economic activity, too, it seems entirely reasonable to expect that the commitment of many creative minds to the formulation and testing of new proposals should bring the benefit of more rapid progress. The market economy has large numbers engaged in making proposals; and the proposals are confined to small sectors and time segments of the whole economy. In such circumstances it is unsurprising that we expect a high chance of superior proposals.

Trial and Error

Motivation, too, is higher where people are in direct pursuit of their private objectives. The man who makes his proposal in the market economy does so in the knowledge that his fate is bound up to some degree with his proposal. The association of subject and proposal is not as close as that between subject and mutation in evolutionary development, for the unsuccessful businessman will not perish with his proposal; but the association is there because success will bring increased fulfillment of economic aims. In short, people are committed to their economic proposals because they stand to gain or lose according to the success or failure they achieve.

In a centrally directed economy it is often the case that there is no such close association: people carry out directives from the central controlling authority and have little incentive to make successful proposals, even in the limited cases in which they are permitted to. To establish motivation, the central authority has to set nominal targets for participating individuals, targets whose attainment will bring fulfillment of private objectives. Thus there is the device of the production bonus, which is paid to sectors of the economy that fulfill production quotas. The attempt is to tie what the authority wishes to be achieved (a certain level of production) to what the individual wishes to achieve (greater purchasing power or more leisure time). The factory owner in a market economy has incentive to supply what consumers require because he will directly gain his ends by doing so; in a directed economy some artificial link must be supplied.

Successive collectivizations in Soviet agriculture have whittled the size of the permitted private plot to an average half-acre. On the rest of the land the agricultural economy is centrally directed, and the farm worker produces for fixed wages what he is told to produce. On the private plot he produces what he wants to produce, and is permitted to keep what is produced. Private plots occupy 3 percent of all Russian cultivated land, yet yield almost half the milk and meat, three-quarters of the eggs, and two-thirds of the potatoes produced in the Soviet Union.[15] Motivation is not a factor which can be lightly ignored.

In the market situation we saw that individual competitive proposals and inadequacy elimination translated into a convergence by the system toward consumer satisfaction. That is, the effect of an inadequate proposal is to produce a situation in which a more adequate replacement will be substituted. More bluntly still, we might say that those who make good proposals tend to get the rewards at the expense of those who do not make good proposals (and "good" is measured by the propensity to satisfy consumers). The market thus continually channels resources away from people who have made unsuccessful proposals and toward those who have shown, by contrast, the ability to satisfy consumer preference. The centrally directed system does not do this. Even if, despite all the difficulties attending the lack of adequate comparison, inferior proposals are detected, there is no mechanism whereby resources are directed away from their perpetrators and into the hands of those who propose more successfully. The planned system, however, has a rough equivalent whereby the results of trials are fed into subsequent proposals, and this is the purging of economists who make incorrect predictions. Unfortunately for the efficiency of the system, this replacement of personnel is often made at levels other than those where the mistakes were made, and carries no guarantee that the successors will be any better. The market replaces a bad guesser by a better one; the planned system might easily replace the bad guesser by one equally bad, if it manages to replace him at all.

In view of the fact that fewer conjectures and marketing tests are made under the planned system, it would appear probable that since less information is gained from mistakes, there also will be less opportunity to gain information concerning possible new products. In the same way that we described a conjecture as "fertile" if it inspired tests which could lead to proposals in other fields, there is a parallel in economic activity. Economists talk of the "spin-off" when work on the creation or improvement of one product leads to unanticipated ideas concerning new products. Development of a new type of plastic for one product, for example, has often led to suggestions for its use to improve another, totally different product. The alloy devised for an airplane might find its way into the engine of a motor car; the material devised to solve problems associated with space travel might also be used as the coating on a nonstick frying pan. When the effort of improvement attempts is spread widely, so that thousands of firms and individuals attempt to improve products, we are more likely to receive unexpected "fallout" benefits of progress in other sectors than when production is controlled by an overall plan.

It appears from the foregoing considerations that the market economy is more conducive to progress than its planned counterpart. In every aspect of competitive proposal and testing for elimination it produces conditions more susceptible to rapid and convergent progress toward the aims of those participating. Only in the objectives of the ruling authority of a planned economy does the directed system achieve what they would call progress. And even in these cases there is the serious drawback of an absence of effective comparison. There are good reasons for supposing that even these objectives could be achieved more rapidly and more effectively by the market-type economy if the authorities were prepared to enter it as participants, bidding sufficiently high for their objectives. Such a situation would have all the advantages of motivation, multiplicity of competing proposals, effective testing of alternatives, and elimination of less adequate procedures. Neil Armstrong remarked, on his way to the moon, that it gave little comfort to reflect that his safety depended upon the operation of millions of parts, *all built by the lowest tender.* He did not remark that the mobilized resources of a sophisticated planned economy had failed to achieve what private motivation and individual proposal and elimination achieved. The United States government achieved its objectives in space research by entering the market as a bidder and letting the market economy progress toward the objective by competitive attempts.

While the market economy is an efficient device for the achievement of the individual, self-referring ends of its participants, and for attaining what may, because of general acquiescence, be regarded as the collective ends of society, it is not the vehicle best equipped to advance toward those aims which people hold concerning the behavior of others. Adam Smith used the metaphor of the "Invisible Hand" which somehow contrives to direct self-seeking activities into the service of the common good.[16] Our analysis enables us to put the same thought in more rational terms, and say that in a market situation the fulfillment of private ends requires that goods and services be supplied which consumers would rather possess than the resources necessary for the fulfillment of those ends. People will part with their resources if they prefer the goods or services to the continued possession of those resources; thus the man who supplies those goods or services is enabled to accumulate the resources required for his own objectives. He has to satisfy "the common good" in order to achieve his ends; hence the "Invisible Hand."

It is entirely conceivable, however, that moral ends may be sought by individual members of society which are not served by the self-referring objectives of others. For example, someone whose aim is a society in which men are equal in their material possessions will not find the market economy is conducive to advancement toward that end. Because he has objectives which are at a superior level in the hierarchy of motivations to economic aims, he will not be able to describe the convergence on private fulfillment as "progress." An essential facet of the market economy is disparity of achievement. It is this very disparity which serves as the guide for the rejection of inferior alternatives; if every attempt brought the same result, there would be no basis for the elimination of some alternatives. Nor would there be motivation for experimental proposal and testing. Nor would there be reason for emulation of either performance or achievement. Disparity of achievement is fundamental to the operation of the system; it is the basis of measurement that some ways are better than others. Without it there could be no progress toward fulfillment of private economic ends.

The visible disparity is undoubtedly a focus for discontent and a source of envy: this is part of its value to progress. Contented people do not make progress, for they have no need to. Advancement toward aims necessarily implies unfulfilled objectives. The contented man, being satisfied, has no concept of a superior ideal, no hypothetical level of attainment with which to compare his actual level. Envy and discontent are the driving forces which lead men to seek progress. Advancement requires motivation, as well as method, and it is the appreciation that a better state is possible which supplies that motivation. The superior level of possible attainment may either be imagined or it may be seen as an actual achievement by others; in either case it is the dissatisfaction with the present state (which this contemplation arouses) which pushes men into doing something about it. The Elysian dream of the Lotus Eaters is only a dream. Though men yearn for rest and contentment, these are not the attributes of humanity, but of the sheep pen and the quiet pasture. Those who attempt to remove from human society envy and discontent, which are so great a source of unhappiness, are attempting to remove the wellsprings of progress.

It is claimed of the market system of economic organization that it emphasizes the self-seeking rather than the cooperative side of man's nature, that it is only self-interest writ large. While this examination is more concerned with the relative efficiency of the rival systems as vehicles for the achievement of progress, it is well to reiterate the point that the market system harnesses what are admittedly self-seeking ends into the service of consumer satisfaction, as a necessary means of approaching those ends. The market economy is only a type of organization; the ends it reflects are only those of the participating individuals. It may well be that some people would like to prevent others from achieving private ends because they disapprove of those ends, and would like to curtail the operation of the market economy because it allows those ends to be pursued. But this is very different from categorizing the system itself as one which *generates* ends which some think undesirable. The system in fact allows the pursuit of a variety of ends, both social and individual. The desire to make others happy is a possible objective within the market organization, as is the desire for private gain.

In practice, societies with strong market elements in their economic arrangements have found it possible to redress what are considered moral failings in a superior economic system by taking political action outside the sphere of the economic institutions. Thus, because it is considered morally undesirable that some members of society who perform poorly in the market system should be unable to live decent lives, some of the gains of the successful are directed toward the less successful by political action. Again, because gross disparities of material possessions are regarded as potential sources of more unhappiness than society will accept, "progressive taxation" is introduced to redistribute income, to some degree, after disparity of attainment has been recorded. As long as there is sufficient disparity to supply motivation, society is able to enjoy all the advantages of economic progress and yet redress some of the unhappiness which is brought about by the discontent required for that progress. The attempt has been to retain the system which brings advancement toward achievement of more and better and cheaper goods, and yet to take such actions outside that system as will alleviate what are felt to be moral shortcomings. The more resources which are available to a society, the more will it be able to cope with poverty in absolute terms, and the more will it be able to extend the range of choice that is open to its citizens.

The market economy itself is morally neutral. Its function is to provide a framework within which people can pursue their individual economic objectives, whatever they are. Its rewards are not allocated on the basis of moral worth, but only in terms of the value to society of the goods and services offered by the participants. These may be in the form of manual labor, which is relatively easy to obtain, or in the form of creative imagination, which is somewhat more rare. The valuation takes more account of achievement than effort; it is made of the actual worth to society of the goods or services presented, no matter how they are achieved. It follows from this that the market has no sense of human *fairness* imposed on it, as "fairness" can be imposed on a directed economy. In market conditions an utterly "unworthy" person might be able to produce goods and services that are of more value to the rest of the community than those of a more "worthy" person. Whatever our standard of "fairness," the market does not register it, unless "fairness" itself is tied to the notion of economic worth to society.

It is in part a desire to make life "fairer" which leads to the imposition of moral values on an economic system. It seems wrong to many people that a dissolute but popular entertainer should be able, by recording four songs a year, to command resources many times those of the devoted nurse who works hard for more than sixty hours every week, ministering to those in sickness and distress. The singer receives more reward from the market because he supplies a product and service which perhaps millions wish to buy. They part with their money in order to receive the added pleasure brought by his singing. The nurse, on the other hand, though she might be worthier by any moral standard, can minister to a few hundred people at most. The market allocates its rewards by economic valuation; and this is what seems unfair.[17]

A man can gain enormous rewards from the market by virtue of simple luck. If he is so fortunate as to hit upon a product or service in wide demand, he will harvest vastly greater resources than some very worthwhile person who has put in a great deal of effort over a long period but has not had the good luck to achieve a breakthrough. This, too, seems unfair to many people. The desire is very real to establish an economic organization which will reflect valuations of people other than those of economic worth. One advantage of the directed economy is that decisions may be made concerning relative worth which are totally arbitrary in economic terms because they are made by some other standard. In the planned economy the nurse can be paid more than the popular singer. Unfortunately, the abandonment of economic measures means that economic ends will not be fulfilled. Whereas the market economy converges on consumer satisfaction, the rejection of market mechanisms involves a denial of consumer satisfaction. It might seem fair that plumbers, for example, should be paid less than farmers, but any transference of that opinion of fairness into economic terms will immediately dislocate the relative supply of plumbers and farmers. In a market situation, plumbers will command high rewards when there is a shortage of them; and the high rewards will encourage more people to take up plumbing (thus redressing the shortage). In an economy in which plumbers are paid by a noneconomic standard of worth, there will be no incentive for shortages (or surpluses) to be corrected. The alternative to incentive is coercion; but that involves consideration of still more moral issues.

Trial and Error

The market economic system holds more knowledge in its mechanisms than can ever be held simultaneously by any individual or group.[18] It is a form of "epistemology without a knowing subject."[19] A shortage will cause prices to rise, and will encourage both the commitment of resources to produce more of what is in short supply and the use of substitutes to replace it. All of this can happen without anyone being required to know how the shortage came about, or how long it is likely to last. Perhaps only a handful of people know that a tin mine is now exhausted; many, many more will see the consequent rise in tin prices, and many will search for cheaper substitutes or start to tap what were formerly uneconomic tin mines.[20] The market itself produces circumstances in which people behave in such a way as to minimize the effect of the events. No one has to order people to produce more tin or make do with something else; the price mechanism does it instead.

The system converges upon achievement of the aims of the participants because it operates by those aims. They provide the motivation and the basis for tests. If we inspect once more the two-part formula of progress which was arrived at in chapter 2, we can see how neatly it is described in economic terms by the market economy. The formula required (1) agreement on an objective and (2) a procedure of testing for competing proposals, with elimination of the less adequate:

$$A_1 \text{ or } A_2 \to T \to CP \to IE \to A_2.$$

In the case of a private aim pursued individually, we can substitute "clear appreciation of the aim" for "agreement" on it. We can see from the foregoing description of the market economy that its structure allows the efficient operation of both parts of the formula. Its better accommodation to those required conditions explains why it is necessarily the more efficient vehicle of economic progress.

Madsen Pirie

Notes

[1] The point discussed in chapter 2, footnote 16.

[2] There is debate between historians on this. Against the view set out here may be opposed the "McDonagh thesis," that the reforms, although owing something to utilitarian thought, were basically fueled institutionally, and that the setting up of inspectorates to manage the first few reforms acted as a spur to further reforms.

[3] This statement does not, of course, exclude the possibility that events beyond the range of nineteenth-century legislation might have brought greater misery to greater numbers. Booth's report on conditions in London at the turn of the century was one factor contributing to the disappearance of what some have described as nineteenth-century complacency.

[4] This was the case considered briefly in chapter 1.

[5] But even utilitarian theorists recognized that "pain counts for more than pleasure," and one school developed the point to the extent of substituting "minimize pain" for either "maximize happiness" or "achieve the greatest balance of pleasure over pain."

[6] The mercantilists exemplify this view. Because they thought wealth was fixed, they thought that one country could become richer only if others became poorer. Their policies (holding sway in eighteenth-century France in particular) were thus designed to maximize total inflowing wealth and to minimize total outflowing wealth—even if this, unknowingly, stunted economic growth. Their concern was with an increased share of what they thought was a constant trade, rather than with a constant share of an increasing trade. Events of the past decade in Britain have made it clear that mercantilism has by no means disappeared from modern economic thought.

[7] In the example given, it is assumed that no buyer or seller commands a share of the market large enough to influence or personally affect the outcome.

[8] Alternatively, the imposition by law of a price ceiling in times of scarcity will mean that extra resources will not be committed to supply, and allocation of the scarce commodity must be by some form of rationing other than pricing (itself a form of rationing).

[9] It should be understood that the term *competitive market economy* is not used to denote any economy which has, in fact, ex-

isted. It is a theoretical model. It does not represent a situation which can be expected to arise without political intervention, because there are economic forces which, if left alone, militate against competition. If ever a free-market economy has occurred, the probabilities are that it did so by chance, and that it was short lived. To establish and maintain a competitive market economy would require considerable and constant application of governmental power, power our societies have not seen applied to that end.

[10]It is important that monopolies of labor are not omitted from the defects of *laissez-faire* situations. While monopolies of capital or commodities might arouse most opposition, the activities of powerful trade unions can achieve a monopoly of labor far more complete in its effectiveness, and at least as damaging in its consequences.

[11]The efficiency of attempted "coercive" advertising is controversial. Against the arguments of J. K. Galbraith (*American Capitalism* [1952]) and Vance Packard (*The Hidden Persuaders* [1957]) may be set the fate of the Ford Edsel car, whose failure, despite the most modern and sophisticated marketing campaign, has been documented many times; and on the other side is the fact that analysis of advertising shows that it is used primarily for interlopers to break into established markets, rather than for established products to hold their markets.

[12]Some leaders of trade unions have argued that the purpose of production is not and should not be to provide products for consumers, but rather to provide employment for working men. Obviously, if such aims are attempted, convergence will be upon some factor other than consumer satisfaction.

[13]And trade unions represent men as sellers of labor, not as buyers of consumer products (even though they are usually both).

[14]The invention of the ball-point pen, for example, in a very short time made useless all the long-term plans involved in mining the metal which is used for the nibs of fountain pens.

[15]From A. N. Sakoff's "The Private Sector in Soviet Agriculture" (monthly bulletin of *Agricultural Economics,* FAO, Rome, 11/9/1962). Referred to in Ardrey's *Territorial Imperative.*

[16]Adam Smith, *The Wealth of Nations* (1776).

[17]F. A. von Hayek, in his *Studies in Philosophy, Politics and Economics* (1967), distinguishes between "distributive justice" and

"commutative justice." Distributive justice, he says, "is the justice of a command-society or command-economy and irreconcilable with the freedom of each to decide what he wants to do." Commutative justice, on the other hand, rewards by results and not by intentions. It involves not estimating the worth of a person but simply "allowing him to keep what his fellows are willing to pay him for his services."

[18] A point explored by F. A. von Hayek in his essay "The Use of Knowledge in Society," *American Economic Review,* vol. 35 (1945).

[19] The phrase forms the title of one of Popper's essays in *Objective Knowledge* (1972).

[20] Hayek's example.

8
Testing & Social Progress

When attention is extended from the narrow field of economics to the wider progress of man in society, a similar division is encountered between individual and collective ends. Individuals may progress in society by learning how to live in ways which bring increased fulfillment of ends, while societies may be said to advance if their customs and institutions change in such a way that life within them is generally agreed to be better than before. The standard by which "better than before" is judged must be the aims sought by individual members: where there is general agreement, it is because the aim was widely shared. We are considering, then, the increased fulfillment of the objectives of members of society, whether this be achieved by changes in the behavior patterns of the individual or by changes on a large enough scale for them to become the new norms of the society.

For most people, it would probably be true to say that little or no conscious thought goes into the choice of a lifestyle. They unquestioningly adopt the values of the society in which they were raised, and if they are at all aware of alternatives, it is usually in the form of knowing what is done in other countries (or other classes) and regarding it all as remote from, and irrelevant to, their own way of living. What we call "custom" is a major determining factor in the adoption of social values. "We are afraid," said Edmund Burke, "to put men to live and trade each on his own private stock of reason; because we suspect that this stock in each man is small, and that the individuals would do better to avail themselves of the general bank and capital of nations and of ages. Many of our men of speculation, instead of exploding general prejudices, employ their sagacity to discover the latent wisdom which prevails in them."[1]

The customs and traditions of a society are its tested ways of doing things. Something "hallowed by prescriptive practice since time immemorial"[2] is something which has been shown by exhaustive testing to achieve a social aim. There may be better ways of attaining the same objective, or of attaining more objectives, but there is in man what Lord Hugh Cecil describes as "a disposition averse from change," a disposition which he claims "springs partly from a distrust of the unknown and a corresponding reliance on experience rather than on theoretic reasoning; partly from a faculty in men to adapt themselves to their surroundings so that what is familiar merely because of its familiarity becomes more acceptable or more tolerable than what is unfamiliar."[3] There are three distinct notions here, all of which reinforce acceptance of custom: suspicion of the unknown, reliance on experience, and love of the familiar. It is important to realize that they are distinct, and that the familiar is loved because it is familiar,[4] without any necessary regard for its intrinsic merits.

While these notions appear at first glance to militate against social progress, closer inspection shows that they have an important function to play in the service of it. The simple affection generated by familiarity can induce us to prefer the present imperfect to the future perfect because it fulfills an important objective. And although this affection is described as "simple," it is by no means a simple task to account for it. We can see why men should esteem or value the customary for its appreciated merit and utility, but we cannot readily see why they should *like* it. The water shrews which Konrad Lorenz describes in *King Solomon's Ring*[5] learn their little "approved pathways" so that they can move along them at speed, always preferring to keep with the path they know, even when they discover a shorter route. The confusion caused when some small detail of a customary path is disturbed can easily be attributed to the loss of the utility afforded by a known and safe route; but with human beings we are faced with confusion even in cases where there is no apparent utility to be destroyed. An animal, taken from its territory and placed in a new environment, is often subject to fear of the unknown. However, even when it has established that its new surroundings are safe and possess abundant supplies of food, the animal often takes a considerable time before it settles down and can be seen to be "at home" in its new location. It could be that we are watching the results of a relationship to surroundings that is similar to that of humans.

Men, in some way, seem to identify with their environment. It is as if the abstract mind anchors itself in reality by familiarizing itself with the things which surround it. Without regard to any appreciated value they may have, they somehow serve to build identity in the individual, to enable him to feel the confidence of a securely established existence. The security is not the physical security of having access to the means of livelihood and survival, but the security of knowing one's place in the universe. Men furnish their minds with ideas derived from the world about them, and whether this furniture be composed of the ideas of physical objects or the notions of ways of doing things, it serves to fill the mind with the abstractions of observed existence, and gives the mind a character in much the same way that furnishings give character to an empty room. This is the way in which the environment becomes part of a man's identity. The loss of a favorite tree or a familiar shop generates uneasiness because it leaves the mind bereft of part of its familiar furniture, and in a small way threatens the identity an individual has built for himself.

This is no semimystical concept, but is securely based in our knowledge of what constitutes character. We identify other people not only by their physical characteristics but by their "ways of doing things" and, indeed, if we know them at all well, by their "ways of thinking things." As outsiders, we come to recognize the results of a customary mode of mental activity, and we use this recognition to fix a person in our mind and separate and distinguish him from others. Similarly, our awareness of our own identity and distinctiveness is not derived merely from contemplation of our physical body but from a partial appreciation of our own thought patterns. External change, which necessarily leads to loss of the familiar, leaves us so much the less anchored to reality, so much less "identified" in our own eyes.

Ethologists have shown us how, in the animal kingdom, a territorial species is able, within its territory, to defeat an aggressor many times its size and strength.[6] There is little doubt that men, too, derive confidence from being "on their home ground,"[7] that they are more at ease when surrounded by the familiar. This is the "security of identity," referred to above, which enables a man whose individuality is not threatened by the absence of the familiar furniture of his mind to achieve more than one whose mind is disturbed by the problem of having to reestablish himself. It is, I suggest, a transference of the self-love, so important for survival, which brings the affection with which man endows those familiar things that form part of his identity. A man bestows fondness on familiar things because he unconsciously recognizes that, in making up part of his mental identity, they become part of himself. The objects which habitually surround us in the physical world, our ways of doing things, and our ways of thinking things all form part of our unique identity. We feel

Trial and Error

affection for them because they are part of ourselves; thus any deprivation of a habitual sight or sound, or of a traditional mode of behavior, will induce a pang of regret at losing something we love. It is a part of our own self.

Oakeshott tells of the Masai tribe in Kenya,[8] who, when moved from their old surroundings to a new reserve, promptly christened all the hills, plains, and rivers in their new environment after the old ones they had left. By this device they were able to preserve something of the customary, some part of their threatened identities, until they could slowly secure themselves by contemplating and accustoming themselves to the new. History abounds with similar examples. A glance at any atlas will show how in many parts of the world a transplanted people sought to secure identity by carrying with them whatever they could retain of the old. Not only *New* York, *New* Zealand, *New* Jersey, but Cambridge, Birmingham, and Boston testify to the struggle for retention of identity in a changing world.

Much is said of "alienation," as if it were unique to the twentieth century. In fact, men have been "alienated" wherever they have been uprooted from place or habit. The partial loss of identity which comes with the loss of the mind's familiar furniture, and the uneasiness and lack of confidence which accompany this loss, have beset men in every age. Our own century, with its accelerated rate of progress, perhaps throws this problem into sharper relief, but our obsession with it springs partly from our inane belief that to have supplied a new name means to have described a new problem. Men have always been alienated when their identity was threatened, and have dealt with it by retaining what they could of the customary—and proceeding slowly so that they could begin to anchor themselves in the new before they lost sight of the old. By accepting necessary change slowly and a little at a time, men can be assured of having, at any time, an overwhelming preponderance of customary and familiar mental furniture, into which they can incorporate the small elements of the new. Only the advent of too many would-be social reformers, impatient for the millennium within their lifetime, has brought about the rejection of too much of the familiar and the comfortable for people to hold fast to their sense of identity and security.

Love of the familiar for its own sake may thus be seen as a species of self-love, a driving force in the pursuit of such unconscious objectives as the desire for identity and for the security it brings. Love of the familiar, on the other hand, for its merit and utility, is as powerful a sentiment, beckoning us in the same direction. Both reinforce the commitment to testing, as opposed to abstract reasoning. The advantage of a tested way is that its worth is "tangible"; we know that it works. While deductive or inductive calculation might purport to show us the way to superior attainment of our objectives, the tested alternative has *already* shown us its ability. Faith in the tried and trusted familiar, rather than in the planned and calculated unknown, is as old as man. All of our folk proverbs on the subject are among the most familiar. "A bird in the hand is worth two in the bush" bespeaks a caution founded on long experience and sings a sad cynicism of promised tomorrows. The here-and-now has overwhelming advantage over what is merely proffered or predicted: we *know* it is ours. The bird in the hand is secure; and however much better it may be to have two birds, however much richer it may make our lives, however much our pleasure and happiness may be increased, *they* are in the bush. And any opening of our hand to ensnare them may only release the bird we have. Thus the first thing which can be said about the value of a tested alternative is that we know we are in possession of that value, whatever it is.

Closely allied with the fact that we derive actual enjoyment of the here-and-now is the fact that we feel much more competent to quantify the value of something if we have had long ex-

Trial and Error

perience of it. Not only do we know that we enjoy it, we are in a position to estimate *how much* we enjoy it. It has been our experience of the world that has led us to propose that this calculation can be performed more accurately for the practical than for the theoretical. We have observed that there are always more results and consequences of our actions than those we intend.[9] The merit of something which has been with us for a long time may perhaps be estimated from our continual experience of it. The merit of an untested proposal may be computed theoretically, but we know, in making the computation, that there are hundreds, perhaps thousands, of factors which could make our estimate wildly wrong. If, then, we seek to replace something of value by a new thing of greater value, our suspicions arise that the new thing may not be of greater value at all. We may, in fact, be depriving ourselves of a known value in order to replace it with nothing at all. "I returned and saw under the sun that the race is not to the swift, nor the battle to the strong, neither yet bread to the wise, nor yet riches to men of understanding, nor yet favour to men of skill; but time and chance happeneth to them all."[10]

The suspicion concerning the power of man's calculation, this knowledge that things rarely turn out as we intend them, should not lead us to conclude that there is irrationalism in the approach to progress. There may be, but it is not constituted by suspicion. On the contrary, this caution we refer to has often been dignified by the name of "rational prudence." Human nature is pessimistic concerning the ways of men because there is good reason to be so. Man has noted, from his experience, that more factors are involved in human behavior than can ever be taken account of in calculation. He knows that even the most plausible-sounding proposals can come to grief on the rocks of unintended consequence; and his rationalism is cautious because he knows its limitations.

It is not difficult to trace the source of this accusation of irrationalism which is sometimes leveled. There are circumstances in which man will prefer to keep with traditional ways of doing things even when all reason seems to point toward their modification or abandonment. The crux of the matter is, however, that human nature is suspicious not only of man's ability to produce workable plans, derived from abstract reasoning, but suspects man's ability to analyze competently his existing institutions and traditions. The world seems to be inhabited by people who sometimes act stupidly, and who sometimes think stupidly. Our experience has taught us that men are more prone to stupidity in thinking than in acting. We recognize that the man who *thinks* has little to lose, whereas the man who *acts* is committing his fate to his ideas.[11] In any conflict between the ways of men and the thoughts of men, we usually prefer to be guided by what men have actually done, even where the reasoning behind the action eludes us. If men have done things in a particular way for a long time, we are inclined to suppose that there is probably merit in it. The analyst might try in vain to discover what it is that gives the traditional way its superiority. To many people it is enough that it works. If it has been done for a long time, they take it on trust that there are good reasons for it, preferring to count the experience of others a surer guide than their "own private stock of reason."

Even when men of speculation fail to discover latent wisdom in general prejudices, it seems more reasonable to suppose that the power of analytic reasoning is at fault than that a large part of mankind should have been mistaken for so long a period. The bank and capital of nations and ages is the collective experience of mankind; it is the results of many tests by many persons in many periods. It does not seem irrational that men should be less ready to consign the populations of previous ages to the category of fools than to consign some overvaunting abstract reasoner to the category of men lacking wisdom.

Trial and Error

It is not necessary and inevitable to propose that the men of old always knew best, that they were somehow superior to modern man. It is simply that there were more of them, and that they operated (collectively) over a long period. Man assumes that if an institution or a manner of behavior has long been traditional, it is because of its latent value, even where such value is not discerned. He thinks it probable that there is such merit, and in cases of doubt prefers to act on this assumption until evidence leads him to change it. Aware of the risks of acting (as opposed to mere thinking), man puts the onus of proof on the shoulders of those who propose innovations. He does not have to justify his adherence to tradition, because he knows his reasoning may be inadequate for the task. He knows it works, and that it has passed down to him as a tradition because of its proven ability in practice. It has been tested, and has not yet been rejected in favor of an alternative shown to be superior at achieving his social objectives. He asks of innovations that they, too, be tested, so he will have a basis for decision.

The obvious objection to this approach—namely, that it appears to make progress difficult—is no deterrent. The words of another popular proverb come to mind, that "it is better to be safe than to be sorry." Men in general seem to prefer the continuation of traditions which might be valueless rather than risk losing any hidden value they might possess. In some societies, for example, there has been a custom that people should not eat meat from the pig. Although long derided as useless, the tradition was shown to have value when it was discovered that various parasites which prey on the pig can also prey on humans. Thus the tradition of not eating pigs served to keep people free from the infection of these parasites, even though many who subscribed to the custom were undoubtedly unaware of its value. Now that modern hygiene and medical research have done much to remove this danger, the tradition is nonetheless kept in some societies because it is relatively harmless, and because people see no reason to submit themselves to the upset its abandonment would cause. Not only may there still be hidden value in its strict observance, there is also the simple affection for the tradition which was considered above. As was suggested then that the contemplation of the customary and familiar serves to establish and to sustain the individual's identity, it might also be argued that it is in the keeping of their collective customs and traditions that a people builds and sustains its cultural identity.

It is not only affection for the familiar and esteem for the latent value of the traditional which conspire to lead us in the direction of a preference for tested ways, there is also the factor of simple indolence. People not only like the established ways, they not only think them safer, they also find them easier. The easiest way is not found by calculation, for calculation does not come easily. It is the way which can be followed without thought, the customary way. If the old way is adequate, and has been shown to be so from continued usage, then people will continue with it because they cannot be bothered to attempt a new way. A man draws on the "bank and capital" not only because it contains more resources than his own but because it is less burdensome to do so. The individual does not wish to submit himself to a life of worry and perplexity when he could be at ease. The difficulties and the dangers of constant decision making can be avoided by following practices which have been subjected to improvement and refinement over a long period. By drawing on the effort of previous generations, a man is able to put *his* effort into the enjoyment and appreciation of what is already available, and of what he knows he can derive satisfaction from.[12]

Thus there are three strong characteristics which militate against the rejection of tested alternatives. The desire for secure identity, for the latent merit of traditions, and for an easier life—all are factors which incline us to respect the

Trial and Error

customary, proven ways. It might be expected from the foregoing examination that man would always oppose social change. But it does not happen like this. Man recognizes that change is necessary in a changing world. New institutions, ideas, and religions are created; alterations in climate and geography, as well as in agriculture and technology, mean that conditions change; and men must conform their behavior to the new conditions. What was adequate at one time need not be so at another. The latent value of a tradition might depart with the changed external circumstances we encounter. The three factors influence the way in which the behavior of man in society changes. They place a premium upon testing, and upon the demand for rigorous comparison before one way is rejected for another. They militate in favor of gradualism in social change. By changing gradually, as part of a continuous process, we are able to satisfy all three desires to some extent. We give ourselves time to anchor ourselves in the new before the old has been finally discarded; we enable ourselves to reverse course without too much damage if the implementation of new proposals reveals unsuspected and unacceptable consequences; we can slowly fall in with new ways of doing things without the worry that our decisions are irreversible.

The force which generates new social proposals is awareness of inadequacies; and since the notion of "adequacy" is dependent upon an objective, we can say that innovative proposals will be sought whenever people realize that what is achieved falls too short of what is possible. Thus the stimulus might come from a new conception of what is possible (such as might be induced by contemplation of other societies or by an extrapolation of trends within an existing society), or from the impact of new circumstances under which the customary ways achieve fewer objectives than before. A higher target or a lower performance level inculcates a sense of the inadequacy of present practices. When a society's manner of living presents no awareness of inadequacies, we do not expect to encounter much consideration of alternatives. It might be a lack of external examples, or lack of basic changes in circumstances; either way, it means that the impetus which moves men to propose innovations is absent.

Traditions tend to be modified or abandoned by societies only when it is realized that following a custom does not bring satisfactory consequences; and this realization usually takes place over an extended period of time. We might recall from our discussion of such activities as skills and economic systems that the innovator is not only the man who proposes new ways of doing things but the man who proposes new target levels. He is in some sense discontented, for such aspects of the results of traditional behavior leave him dissatisfied.

Social innovations, too, start as minority practices. They start by being the practices of the discontented man and the circle of family and friends he is able to influence directly. Their aim is to achieve results which differ from those produced by the prevailing mode of behavior, and results which are (in their eyes, at least) in some way better and more worthy of being preferred. If they follow their chosen course of behavior, they (and others) will be able to observe the results which actually ensue. If the required consequences are not achieved, then the behavior may be modified in light of the observed difference between the achieved and the intended. That is, new proposals will be sought to close the gap. It sometimes happens that while the result is not what was intended, it is found to be more satisfactory than the results of traditional behavior; so the new way of living may be preferred over the old, even though it failed to achieve the objective.

It is true, of course, that people at times show remarkable resistance to learning from their mistakes in lifestyle, and it may easily come about that the experimental group will persist in its inferior ways even when the results are seen. Whether from pride or ideological commitment, its persistence will not affect the way in which outsiders can learn from the mistakes.

Trial and Error

If the way is no good, they will not follow it, and it will be retained only by the original group and the ever-decreasing group of their descendants who do not abandon it.

On the other hand, if the new method is seen to bring beneficial results to the experimental group, it will be copied by others who wish to take advantage of these benefits. The emulation will be gradual, for people will wish to be as sure as possible, to see it thoroughly tested, and to phase out their reliance on previously adopted ways at a rate that will allow them to accustom themselves to the new. We often see traditions change while retaining their outward form. People gradually switch to new ways while continuing to pay lip service to the old. In this way they retain the "familiarity" aspect of the old until the new is also familiar. When the tradition that is being replaced is no more than an empty shell of public show, and most people have committed themselves to the reality of the new, the old tradition falls quietly into desuetude.

It might be said that people seek the "best" way of achieving social objectives, just as they do scientific or economic objectives—where "best" is unattainable in absolute terms, and only to be achieved as a "best" of currently available alternatives. As with the other fields, it is a continual progress toward an unattainable ideal. As each improvement is adopted as a behavior pattern, it becomes the base for a subsequent further improvement. Since there are no arbitrary conventional goals in social life, we find a hierarchy of ends, with lesser objectives serving more basic ones. In social activities, therefore, we again have the problem of a changing measuring rod; we test and modify our aims, as well as our attempts to achieve them. Changes in aims occur in society in much the same way as changes in behavior. A minority group which has chosen to live by new values can show others, by its success or failure, whether the aims are worth adopting.

There are two sources of complexity. In the first case, it is by no means clear whether what outsiders regard as superior results of a lifestyle are always the consequences of improved behavior toward existing ends or the replacement of those ends by ones which better serve higher objectives. Since the measuring rod against which performance is rated is itself susceptible to alteration, it is difficult to distinguish a change in performance from a change of measure. The second complicating factor is that since people do not necessarily share objectives, the adoption of an aim by one person to satisfy a higher objective might not necessarily mean that another person would find that aim equally satisfying. In both of these cases the resolution of these difficulties is brought about only by testing. It is only by trying it for himself that a person can judge whether he will benefit from the new proposal. The possibility that some innovations will not be susceptible of widespread emulation with the same degree of success affords yet another reason for esteeming the caution with which men proceed toward social change.

Of course, there are many practical objections to the working of so simple a model of social progress. Members of society do not inhabit individual moral islands. To some extent, almost any decision on social life will have its effect on others. Societies show considerable reluctance to allow individuals and groups within their midst to pursue alien lifestyles. It is part of the value of a tradition, for example, that it be accepted by everyone. It was elevated into a tradition only because people found that its keeping produced desirable consequences. If there are now in society people behaving in a different way (and perhaps seeking different ends), then the assurance is gone which used to accompany the tradition. No longer can it be accepted with confidence; people now have to reflect that it might be inadequate. Further, it is established behavior patterns which enable people to predict how others will respond: traditions give people a reasonable basis for day-to-day planning in their relations with others. If some members of society start to live in different ways, then the reasonable

Trial and Error

expectation of the others will be denied, and life for them will become somewhat more confusing and complicated, as the traditional behavior no longer produces the expected result. It is often upsetting for people to see their values overrun. Identification with the traditions and practices of the community can be shaken by the spectacle of nonadherence to what were thought of as basic values. The temptation is great in any society to remove this cause of unhappiness and insecurity by outright prohibition of alternatives which appear to flout the beloved familiar. Finally, it is quite possible that most people would prefer to live by unquestioned traditions, opting to avoid the intellectual ferment in which the values by which they lived were constantly under challenge, and deliberately warding off the unpleasant state of having to think things out for themselves.

These factors represent considerable forces of inertia in a society, forces which could easily be applied to the suppression of new proposals and trials, even in a society which thought of itself as free. They are pressures which could be brought to bear without legal sanction. Withdrawal of goodwill, expression of contempt, and removal of rewards are measures which provide disincentive for social experiment. Society is enabled, by the use of such measures, to add weight to the balance pan and swing it toward prevailing norms. Anyone who experiments with proposed innovations must start by accepting all of these factors in the list of undesirable consequences. Even in a society with no legal bar to social experiment, the pressures to conform socially can be overwhelming. Desire for the respect of one's peer group appears to be a very common (and probably instinctive) motive; thus the deliberate use of that respect, or its withdrawal, is a very powerful weapon in the fight to preserve social norms.[13]

Where legal sanctions are used to interdict experiment with alternative proposals, society is denied the possible benefit gained by comparison of results. When consequences cannot be inspected by testing, members of society have no rational ground for preferring some alternatives to others on the basis of superior performance. Social progress in such circumstances can only be made by chance, through the arbitrary imposition of behavior patterns. Moreover, since there are no alternative experiments taking place within society, the community will be dependent upon external example to supply it with new conceptions of achievement.

It is no accident that an ideological commitment to a particular lifestyle as "necessarily superior" usually involves the total prohibition of alternatives. If individuals and groups are allowed to differ, they might seriously embarrass the ideology by living lives which others regard as more satisfactory than their own. Only by preventing people from following any other path can an ideologically committed society take steps to ensure the preservation of its chosen manner of living. It is notorious, too, that societies which are ideologically committed to particular lifestyles take very good care to ensure that contact with other societies is kept to a minimum. Only by filtering information concerning different societies can those who impose the ideological pattern prevent alternative achievement levels from being conceived and sought. Thus we expect that an ideologically committed society will be characterized by severe limitation on foreign travel for its citizens, careful control of visitors from abroad, the jamming of foreign broadcasts, and the prohibition of foreign publications. Only by steps such as these can possibly embarrassing comparisons be avoided.

In a free market of social proposals, unsatisfactory conjectures pile up like unwanted goods in the windows, with few, if any, customers. People take only the social proposals which will enable them to advance further toward fulfillment of their aims—much as they select goods on the basis of their ability to satisfy economic aims. When only state-produced goods can be bought and sold, people will buy and sell state-produced

Trial and Error

goods. When only state-permitted ideologies are allowed, people will live by them. As with state-monopoly goods, they will have few ways of evaluating the performance of state-monopoly ideology. In the absence of alternatives, they have no way to assess them. If experiment is prohibited, and foreign example is carefully screened away, the only basis of comparison will be previous performance. Periodically, the citizens of such a society might be aware that they are fulfilling aims better or worse than they used to do.

The main drawback of societies which impose legal sanctions on alternative experiment is that the basis for progress is denied. Only one proposal is tested at a time in each section of social life, and when the consequences are found unsatisfactory by comparison with what has been achieved before, or, more likely, with what people were led to expect by the proponents of the ideology, there is no way except the political in which dissatisfaction can be registered. Whereas in a society which allows experiment, people are able to reject the behavior patterns which brought unsatisfactory results and to adopt a proposal which seems to have achieved better results for those who tried it, in the restricted society they have to change the minds of the authorities, or change the authorities.

Social progress in societies which prohibit alternatives tends to be made (if at all) in a series of spasmodic jerks as the pressures of discontent build up to a point where alteration is forced. Testing occurs on only one proposal at a time, and the only basis for comparison is previous or promised performance. There is no smooth process of social transition, no retention of the familiar until men have accustomed themselves to the new, no cautious testing and adoption by emulation. On the contrary, such societies necessarily commit themselves wholeheartedly to a proposal, deriving none of the benefits of gradualism. When a proposal is found wanting, it must be replaced abruptly by a new, wholehearted commitment to a new proposal.

The Russian nobleman who described the tsarist system as "absolutism tempered by assassination" perhaps spoke more wisely than he knew. In the absence of any other means of changing the social state, the last resorts of a people *are* revolution and assassination. If progress is made as a result of comparative testing and inadequacy elimination, and the mechanisms of state do not allow for the testing of alternative proposals, then for progress to take place there must be periodic upsets to the mechanisms of the state. These periodic upsets serve to introduce new styles of living, which soon face the same problems. The process reminds one of nothing so much as the periodic lifting of the lid as pressure builds up inside a kettle. When the steam has escaped, the lid descends until the pressure again builds up to the critical limit. We might note, in passing, that the tsarist system the nobleman referred to was much more pluralistic than many present-day ideologically committed societies.

Pluralistic societies, that is, those which permit experiment with alternative social behavior and values, not only preserve thereby the conditions required for progress, they maintain, in addition, dynamic stability. Because the process of change can be fitted into the internal structure of the society, it can happen smoothly and gradually, without dramatic upset to the whole society. The social values of pluralistic societies are subject to continuous change because people can adopt tested alternatives whenever they are convinced their objectives would be more fully realized by such a move. While very many social experiments are not taken up generally, the potential for change is always present should a superior proposal be revealed by testing. Societies which prohibit alternatives are more stable in one sense, that they go for longer periods without change. But this is the "stability" of building up pressure, as in our kettle analogy. When change comes, it comes violently and at large cost to the society's fabric.

Change must come, too, because of changing circumstances. A society would find it very difficult to immunize itself against all the factors which conspire to make its prevalent lifestyle no longer adequate. Obviously, both technological and economic advance are factors which can influence the effectiveness of established behavior patterns. Both can bring a change in the values by which that behavior is rated. Economic advance can change attitudes to both property and poverty. Stealing a sheep, for example, might be a serious crime in a society where the sheep is the major source of a family's livelihood; it inevitably becomes less serious when economic change means that a sheep is one of a herd of thousands that are reared for profit. Slavery can be regarded as necessary by a society until both technological and economic progress enable it to afford the luxury of regarding slavery as abhorrent.

While an ideologically committed society might conceivably be prepared to forego economic and technological advance in order to preserve its customs, there are some factors over which it has no control. A change in the conditions of life, in the environment itself, can lead to the adoption of new ways as the old ones prove no longer viable. All of the different communities which sought to preserve their values and ethics by emigrating to America were forced, one by one, to face the realities of the new environment and to adopt new standards and ways of behaving.[14] But change comes, in addition, from the growth of knowledge within a society, from accidental discoveries, from the emergence of new religions. All of these would have to be controlled by a society determined to preserve its norms. The task is impossible, for there are too many factors beyond human control.

We might regard these changes as serving the role equivalent to that of the new information in science, which makes us doubt the effectiveness of our models. The new "external" factors which impinge upon our social life are the analogous spur to progress. It is the arrival of these new factors which in some way renders obsolete the old scheme of values. We realize that our existing standards are less effective at achieving social aims; and this is where the innovator steps in with his proposals. Just as we find at the comparable stage in scientific discovery that there are often many people working on the attempt to produce a viable proposal, so, in our social life, we find that when it becomes obvious that traditional ways must be changed, many different solutions are offered to society by different people. And the decision between these conflicting alternatives is made on the basis of testing. We see how people fare who live in these proposed manners, and adopt the ones which produce results corresponding closer to our idea of success. Only rarely in our social life, however, does it become "obvious" that traditions must be changed: an awareness diffuses slowly outward through society from the experimental group in the normal course of social progress. Very infrequently do we find any sudden and dramatic rejections of prevailing lifestyles.

It is this profusion of possible alternatives which John Stuart Mill regards as the key to the success of European culture. "What," he asks, "has made the European family of nations an improving instead of a stationary portion of mankind?"[15] It is not, he tells us, "any superior excellence in them" but "their remarkable diversity of character and culture." In his judgment, "Europe is . . . wholly indebted to this plurality of paths for its progressive and many-sided development." He thinks that it is the large number of ready alternatives which has enabled Europe to advance. When one particular path has been rendered inadequate by a change in circumstances, there have been other ways, already tested in practice, for people to turn to. Mill's view reinforces what we expect from our appreciation of the elements of scientific activity: a solution is more likely to be found if many people are working on the problem in different ways. If a large number of research workers are attempting a variety of alternatives, we rate highly the probability of proposals more successful than existing ones making their appearance. What applies to science applies to social life: the quantity and diversity of the simultaneous experiments give us more chance of meeting superior proposals.

It is remarkable that the achievements of European culture should have become the standard by which, all over the world, progress is measured. Every other culture has looked at the fruits of European development and resolved to acquire them for itself. We have only one model of "modernity"; it is that of the industrialized growth economy which has characterized the European achievement.[16] As rapidly as they denounce Europe, the other parts of the world strive to emulate her. Our sociologists bewail the wholesale submergence of alternative cultures as everyone rushes to board the European express: as we glibly talk about the need to preserve the "integrity" of other cultures, they rush to adopt, instead, what they regard as a superior manner of living. The European example has set a level of attainment which has become identified with progress. While other cultures might preserve their heritage as tourist attractions, the attempt is always to strive for the "modern" world of the industrialized, mass-production and mass-consumption economy. The attitude of Europeans is notably ambivalent. They talk at once of Europe's mission to help the rest of the world advance, and of the need to regard alien cultures as "equal but different." If the other cultures really were "equal," there would not be the rush to reject them. Our development experts dash around the world sowing dragons' spawn, and then complain that all they produce are more dragons. The facts (whether sad or no) are that European behavioral proposals have produced something that everyone wants. The rest of the world is making progress by emulation, just as progress is made *within* a society by the general spread of the most successful practices.

The pluralism makes not only for Mill's "progressive and

many-sided development" but for safety. A society which has alternatives being tested within it is more resilient to changed circumstances, more ready to survive by adaptation. A society which has long followed a traditional pattern and which does not have alternative examples may disintegrate under the impact of dramatically changed circumstances, much as some primitive societies have collapsed under the impact of European culture. In times of dire stress and emergency, the pluralistic society has a range of alternatives already under test. The new conditions themselves might bring about the dominance of one of these, by supplying the external conditions under which it becomes "superior" (i.e., preferable). Thus as well as supplying a continual threat to established values, the experimental groups provide a kind of safety in diversity.

As H. L. A. Hart has pointed out, there is a kind of arrogance in those who insist that all others are to follow one chosen path.[17] The assumption on their part is that they are in a position to *know* the best way, and that all other paths must necessarily be inferior. Such knowledge is impossible. We are dealing with the products of the human creative imagination as comparatives. There are "better" ways which emerge by testing, but no theoretical "best" way. Only testing reveals which ways are preferable in practice, and there remains the ever-present possibility that a new creative act will produce a proposal that is found more preferable still. It is precisely the impossibility of this sort of knowledge which provides F. A. von Hayek with the basis of his argument for liberty. Since we can never know for certain that any way is correct (we would say "more adequate than its rivals"), Hayek concludes that we should let people pursue their own roads; they may be right, and we wrong.

The implication of this discussion is that we should permit experiment with alternatives for practical reasons, to enable society to be in a better position to cope with any change in circumstances. Mill points out that "although at every period those who travelled in different paths have been intolerant of one another, and each would have thought it an excellent thing if all the rest could have been compelled to travel his road, their attempts to thwart each other's development have rarely had any permanent success, and each has in time endured to receive the good which the others have offered."[18] Although we need not accept Mill's apparent claim that every society has something to offer, we can see that his kind of tolerance gives society the ability to pick the best features from a variety of lifestyles within range of its inspection.

If it is possible to abstract from a particular manner of living those elements of behavior which conspire to produce the part of the result which is agreeable, then a society which has within it a profusion of lifestyles will be able to adopt the best practices from each, in order to make up its "most preferred way." Examples spring readily to mind in which particular elements of behavior have been adopted by a society from one of its subgroups, without the whole package being swallowed. The contribution of Methodism to British society is a good example of this effect, but there are many examples of what is a continual effect in pluralistic societies. The effect has its close parallel in scientific discovery, where it sometimes comes about that even though a proposal be rejected, elements in it are found worthy of incorporation into subsequent proposals because of their ability to extend our predictive power. Planck's quantum theory contains elements of both Huyghens's wave theory and Newton's corpuscular theory, neither of which was, by itself, able to serve as a satisfactory model.

Progress in social life consists in the adoption of proposals which enable us to approach nearer to social objectives. The pluralistic society allows for independent proposal and independent testing of innovations. It enables the rest of society (other than the experimental groups) to have access to testing results without putting itself at risk. By accepting the occasional distress which is caused by minority groups rejecting established values, the rest of society can observe experiments in which its own fate is not tied to the success or failure of the proposals under test. If there are unacceptable consequences, then only the innovators will suffer them. If the consequences are found desirable by other members of society, they will be able to emulate the innovators at a safe distance behind them. The freedom to propose both new behavior patterns and new objectives is important to the efficient operation of the progress formula. There must be alternatives, and there must be a disparity of achievement between different proposals so that there can be grounds for decision between them.

The cardinal virtue of a democratic system of government is not that it produces the best leaders, or even (as is commonly supposed) that it enables the will of the majority to be put into effect, but that it is the political system most amenable to testing and inadequacy elimination. Few people these days cherish illusions about the quality of leaders produced by democratic states. Some, indeed, argue that better leaders were produced by aristocratic societies, when men tended to emerge who had time to think, and who did not need financial gratification from office. Since Plato's *Republic*, men have been concerned to find ways of selecting the best leaders; political philosophers have thought that the problem was devising ways in which the most noble, educated, altruistic, etc., etc., people could be placed at the head of the body politic.[19] The difficulties discussed were those of discovering or inventing such a system, with implementing it, and persuading the common people to accept this wise and noble leadership, even where it disagreed with their own views. The failure of all these attempts led people to suggest that perhaps no one could ever know which are the best ways, or recognize them if he saw them. One of the arguments commonly adduced for democracy is that it involves a kind of "collective guilt." Since no one knows what is right, it is argued, only by involving everyone in decisions can we produce a situation in which people have no one to blame but themselves.

Rather more pessimistic political philosophers have pointed out that even if there were a system of selecting the best rulers, we would have no guarantee that they would continue to retain the qualities which inspired their selection. It is possible that the very exercise of life-and-death power over millions might induce moral degeneration, might breed arrogance and lead to the imposition of the personal ends of the rulers. Even Marcus Aurelius appointed his own unworthy son as his successor. When Malcolm Muggeridge realized, after his "Winter in Moscow,"[20] that perhaps revolutions are "doomed" to be betrayed, that perhaps the very concentration of power induces its abuse, he was expressing Montesquieu's dictum, made famous by Lord Acton but observable in every age and civilization. The real political question is not how we can select our rulers but how we can tame them.

The point about the democratic system is that we can *change* our rulers. We learn from our mistakes by removing (peacefully) the men who were in charge when the mistakes were made and by replacing them with a group of men committed to trying another way. Their way may also be wrong, but then they, too, can be dismissed in turn. Not only do democratic societies learn from their mistakes, but the leaders have an incentive to be right, or, more accurately, a disincentive to be wrong. Because no leader is installed beyond recall, each one knows that he will be called to account after a specified period. His task, therefore, if he wishes to retain office, is to behave in such a way that voters will prefer him to the alternatives offered. Only by this periodic call to account can society shield itself from the possibly corrupting effects of power. If a leader is corrupted by power, then he can be dismissed. Democratic societies do not always see the will of the majority being implemented. What they see is the verdict of the majority on the relative competence of administrations. If the effects resulting from policies of one administration are felt by the majority to be less adequate than the alternatives might be, the majority can reject that administration in favor of one of the alternatives.

The key facet of democracies is not the "popular mandate" but the periodic call to account. It is not that we can put into power whom we want, but rather that we can turn from power those we do *not* want. Critics of modern Western democracies who claim that the people have no "real" choice are missing the point. Even if two (or more) teams of men stand for the same type of society, it is still beneficial for the achievement of people's objectives that they should be allowed to throw out one set in favor of another. Because the various teams are actively seeking power, they have the incentive to behave in such a way that people will vote them in, and not vote them out. Democracy achieves the shifting of the private objectives of the rulers into the service of the collective aims of the society. To fulfill his objective, the ruler must satisfy the aims of the majority better than anyone else can. Just as in economics the effect of the market system is to make the fulfillment of private ends dependent upon ability to achieve consumer satisfaction, so, in the democratic society, the effect is to make the fulfillment of a desire to attain and keep power dependent upon ability to achieve voter satisfaction. Whereas political philosophers have looked for ways of ensuring that our leaders have worthy motives, the democratic system is able to channel their ordinary motives into the service of the achievement of collective desires. Like the market economy, the democratic system of government is considerably more sophisticated in its operational elements than it appears to be.

Nondemocratic governments have managed to incorporate some of the seemingly attractive elements of democracy into their systems. Authoritarian regimes have enjoyed notable success with the stage-managed plebiscite, and even with "elections," albeit often without alternative choices. But all of this is window dressing without the basic element of the democratic system: the ability to remove rulers peacefully, and thus effect change in the policies being pursued.[21] In the absence of peaceful mechanisms for change, we said, the last resorts of a people are revolution and assassination. It is because revolution is difficult and a source of considerable social distress that it is not a frequent remedy. People will prefer to accept less than adequate ways because the alternative of revolution is even more inadequate. In a democratic society they do not have that terrible choice. Change can be implemented as and when it is felt to be needed, and it can be done within the institutions, and unaccompanied by the total upheaval of society. Thus democratic societies can respond better to changing circumstances, and display at all times more efficient conditions for the achievement by citizens of those aims shared sufficiently widely to become influential in elections.

Democratic societies need not be pluralistic. The phrase "the tyranny of the majority"[22] has at times assumed an ugly meaning. But there is a strong tendency for democracies to encourage pluralism, one which derives from the institutional framework of the system. Because a democracy translates the private aims of the rulers into the service of the objectives of members of society, the ruler is encouraged either to satisfy widely shared objectives or to create conditions in which they can be satisfied. The rulers are more likely to retain power by a favorable verdict from the electors if they have satisfied as many private objectives as possible, including those of minority groups where they do not conflict with the others. This is the process called "building a majority," in which rulers (or would-be rulers) attempt to harness to their political bandwagon the aims of as many minorities as they can. In a highly pluralistic society such as the United States, the art of politics consists, in large measure, of combining minority interests into a political platform. The poor, the blacks, the young, housewives, Jews, veterans—all are courted by politicians who are anxious to build a total vote of support sufficiently large for the attainment and preservation of power. The democratic society tends to be pluralistic because the leaders are constrained by the system into the satisfaction of as many private aims as can be reconciled with each other. Thus the democratic type of society is conducive to progress in minority aims, as it is to progress in the achievement of majority aims.[23]

One advantage, noted in the comparison of economic systems as possessed by the market model, is that it is more likely that inadequacies can be tracked down on the small scale. Where experimental proposals are tested individually, we can attribute consequences to the proposal much more readily than when a huge conjunction of proposals is tested. Similarly in our social proposals, we are far more likely to track inadequacies back to their source when the innovations are proposed individually in response to need, rather than as some block ideological package presented as a panacea. In human behavior we have noted that the complexities are such as always to produce some effects additional to those intended. By making our changes "piecemeal" (as Popper describes it),[24] we are less likely to find our intended reforms leading to an immense series of undesirable changes, since we can check the results as we go along and can relate consequences to individual proposals. Progress by the method of competitive testing and inadequacy elimination is necessarily systematic and gradual. It is systematic because we proceed in stages, always accepting whichever alternative is shown in practice to be better. It is gradual because we advance here and there, now improving one aspect, now another. All of the proposed modifications are tested against each other and against our current practices. Little by little we accept some and discard others, and little by little we advance by the elimination of in-

Trial and Error

ferior choices. If we engage in many changes simultaneously, we shall find ourselves unable to inspect which changes produced which effects, and the efficiency of our testing will be impaired.

If a golfer introduced, all at once, a new stance, a new swing, and a new set of clubs, he would have no way of knowing which of them was critical to the change in his performance. Only by keeping everything else as constant as possible and testing the innovations one by one would he be able to tell which ones were of benefit to his game and which ones were not. When the scientist devises tests for his theory, he spends a great deal of effort *isolating* the factor under test. He tries to keep the behavior of the rest of the "universe" as constant as possible in order that he might test the new factor in isolation, and not merely test the conjunction of an unknown number of unknown circumstances. To assist him in this difficult task he sometimes makes use of the "control group," setting up two experiments which are identical in all respects save one—the one that is influenced by the factor under test. Only in this way can he test the influence of that factor alone.

So is it in our social innovations. If they are tested little by little, with the rest of society's practices held constant, we will be able to attribute change in results to the operation of the innovation. It is more efficient for judging the efficacy of new practices if the groups which introduce them do so in small doses. If a group introduces a completely new lifestyle, one which differs markedly from prevailing norms, it gives us little information for observing the results of its new ways. If unacceptable results are produced (unacceptable, that is, to the rest of society), there is no way of knowing which particular innovations are the ones to be avoided. We cannot progress by testing and inadequacy elimination unless we know which proposals introduce which inadequacies.

It is important that there should be no "privileged" proposals in social innovation. No matter how detailed the analysis of human nature and sociological forces which are claimed to have gone into the formulation of a proposal, it should stand no better and no worse than any other untested proposal. The strength of ideology is a totally irrelevant factor; it does not matter how much some people might *want* particular proposals to be superior at achieving objectives. Once formulated, all conjectures join the ranks of proposals waiting to be tested, and their treatment must be carried out without regard to the degree of faith behind them. It is a simple, undeniable fact that many of the things in which men have believed most strongly have turned out to be totally inadequate. Thinking men once held the conviction that the earth was flat; indeed, they held this belief even more strongly than today's social scientists believe that the "environment" is everything in the makeup of character and personality. The view of the flat earth was not saved by the belief.

We have, in any case, no reason to suppose that those social innovations which claim to derive from calculation are any better than those which admit to being the inspired product of a creative mind. Experience has given us no basis for preferring one type rather than the other. Rejection, modification, or retention takes place only on the basis of testing results, and we certainly have no basis for abandoning the tested proposals which represent society's current practices and values in favor of any plausible but untested scheme of alternatives. Apprehension at the fanciful proposals we are sometimes asked to act upon cannot be dispelled by argument. It is an apprehension founded on suspicion and embittered by practical experience. We have as yet encountered no test which might lead us to abandon the proposal that disaster follows if society commits itself wholesale to the implementation of untested proposals.

Trial and Error

Notes

[1] Edmund Burke, *Reflections on the Revolution in France* (1790).
[2] Burke's phrase.
[3] Lord Hugh Cecil, *Conservatism* (1912).
[4] A distinction amplified by Michael Oakeshott in his *Rationalism in Politics* (1962), essay titled "On Being Conservative."
[5] Konrad Lorenz, *King Solomon's Ring* (1952).
[6] Discussed in N. Tinbergen's *The Herring Gull's World* (1953), Robert Ardrey's *Territorial Imperative* (1966), and Konrad Lorenz's *On Aggression* (1963).
[7] A fact which is illustrated every Saturday in Britain on football grounds all over the country. The side playing "at home" is assumed to have an advantage, even when numbers of supporters are equal. The "home win" is expected; the "away win" is thought less likely. Goals scored "away" count for more than those scored "at home."
[8] In "On Being Conservative" from *Rationalism in Politics*.
[9] A fact which has been widely used in opposition to schools of would-be social planners. Hayek's *Studies in Philosophy, Politics and Economics* makes much of it.
[10] Ecclesiastes 9:11.
[11] In his *Objective Knowledge* Popper shows how our ideas, by being placed into "World III," can compete for survival, without their fate being tied to the organisms which produced them. In evolution, the originator dies if his innovation is no good; in the world of ideas, the originator can survive because his innovations are detached from him, existing autonomously in their World III. The man who *acts* on his ideas is committing his fate to them, and has more at stake than the man who merely *thinks*.
[12] Oakeshott, in his essay "On Being Conservative" (*Rationalism in Politics*), characterizes the conservative as the man who sees opportunities for happiness and satisfaction in *prevailing* conditions, rather than in imagined future states.
[13] Deliberate withdrawal of respect by a peer group may be seen in its extreme form in "sending someone to Coventry." In whatever

group it is used, among schoolchildren, working men, or wives of businessmen, it represents the extremity of social disapproval, and is a device designed to bring the recalcitrant back to conformity while discouraging emulation by others.

[14] A story documented by Daniel J. Boorstin in *The Americans—1: The Colonial Experience* (1958).

[15] John Stuart Mill, *On Liberty* (1859).

[16] J. K. Galbraith says, in his *Economic Development* (1964): "Development is the faithful imitation of the developed." Sidney Pollard makes a similar point in *The Idea of Progress* (1968) when he says: "More interesting, however, is the assumption of the inevitability of 'economic development' in the Western sense, among the large majority of the world's population living in 'underdeveloped' economies" (ch. 5).

[17] H. L. A. Hart, *Law, Liberty and Morality* (1963).

[18] Mill, op. cit.

[19] Popper is, once more, a notable exception. In his *Open Society* (vol. II) he argues that this is the wrong problem. He says: "It forces us to replace the question: 'Who should rule?' by the new question: 'How can we so organise political institutions that bad or incompetent rulers can be prevented from doing too much damage?'"

[20] The essay he wrote after his experiences of visiting the Soviet Union in high hopes, only to appreciate at firsthand the nature of its reality.

[21] It is noteworthy that the decline in the use of impeachment as a political weapon in Britain was accompanied by the increasing dependence of administrations upon a parliamentary majority. When there is an institutional method of opposing policy, or of removing officeholders, there is no more need for the fiction that they are "criminals," to be removed by impeachment. Only in countries where officeholders cannot be so removed are such devices as impeachment still current.

[22] The phrase is from Alexis de Tocqueville's *Democracy in America* (1840).

[23] Indeed, there can be cases where the one is prejudicial to the other in a way inconceivable in authoritarian societies. It has been seriously argued, for example, that United States politicians have

Trial and Error

been forced to pay *too much* attention to minority demands. Because of the balance between the two parties, elections tended to be decided in the so-called "swing states" of the East and Midwest. These states were characterized by large urban minorities of poor, blacks, etc., and so, it has been argued, politicians gave them disproportionate attention. Only with the change of the voting habits of Southern states in the 1960s was the balance shifted away from these "swing states."

[24]In his *Open Society* (vol. II).

9
Optimum Conditions

For progress to take place in any activity, conditions must prevail which satisfy the internal requirements of the system. That is, the two-part formula of progress must be satisfied. There must be clear sight of the aims, a mental concept of what it would be like to succeed. There must be testing of alternative proposals in such a way that we are able to see which one results in a state corresponding most closely to that mental concept. There must be decision, at this critical point in testing, to prefer the alternative which achieves the closest correspondence. These conditions are all "internal" in that they relate directly to the terms in the equation. But there are other conditions which, although not necessarily vital, are certainly conducive to the efficient operation of the method, and appropriate, therefore, to the promotion of progress.

In order for men to make progress, they must desire the nominated aims. This sounds tautological, and for most cases it is, since the aims are what is desired, and they supply their own motivation. There are cases, however, where the end is an arbitrary, conventional one, or a general end not necessarily shared by all individuals; and in these cases additional motivation will be required to attach the private ends of people to the service of the required major objective. In science we saw that even if people do not share the general desire to predict the observed universe (for the power it brings), they can be motivated to scientific research by conventional prizes in the form of financial gain or the respect of their fellow men, or even self-respect. In economics the market system ties the desire for private gain to the satisfaction of consumer preference. In democratic systems of government the desire for achievement and retention of power can be fulfilled by the satisfaction of voter preference. In every case it is a question of supplying external motivating factors to an objective whose satisfaction is thought to bring general good in the form of increased ability to fulfill private aims. From the point of view of progress, there is little to be achieved by stipulating that men *should* pursue these worthwhile motives for their own sake; this is akin to expressing the wish that people were other than they are. This might indeed be pleasant, but the only way, short of coercion, to make men live by motivations other than the ones they feel is to attach their fulfillment to those motivations which men *do* feel.

If there is to be progress, there must be proposals. Conditions must prevail under which men can feel discontented with existing levels of achievement. There must be an awareness that more is possible, an awareness deriving from external example or from extrapolation based on internal criticism. The point has already been made that the creative imagination seems more prone to inspire new proposals when existing ones are being subjected to critical appraisal. There must also be opportunities for testing proposals, for comparing the results achieved by the various alternatives, and for making the decision to eliminate from consideration those proposals (new or old) which produce results less adequate than others at achieving the sought-after objective.

This chapter is concerned with the optimization of the external prevailing conditions in such a way that progress will proceed most efficiently, most rapidly, and yet most safely. It is concerned, then, with the measures which man can take in order to maximize his progress. *Progress* is taken, as before, to mean advancement toward whatever it is he wants to achieve. Man's behavior changes, and man's desires change. With those changes, he is presented new problems at every turn. For his comparative aims, he is presented an unending sequence of problems, the solution of each one being a higher level of performance and attainment than he enjoyed before. But although the problems change, the principles which govern the solutions to those problems do not change; and our concern is with the conditions which underlie those principles.

The first requirement is freedom. People must be allowed to criticize existing achievement levels and to propose alternative aims and behavior patterns. They must be permitted to test, to observe the results of those tests, and to make decisions on the basis of them. Tolerance, therefore, is at a premium in the conditions for progress. A society which not only permits, in law, the right of private dissent but manages to minimize the social pressures working toward total conformity is one which stands to gain from the observation of results achieved by alternative social proposals. The arguments of libertarian philosophers have centered around the morality of freedom,[1] the fact that only through making personal decisions and accepting consequences can people acquire moral worth and responsibility. They have taken as the basis of a political system the dictum of Milton: "If every action which is good or evil in a man of ripe years were under pittance and prescription and compulsion, what were virtue but a name, what praise would be due to well-doing?"[2] and have declared liberty to be the source of all values.[3] The concern herein is with the logic of freedom, not its morality. Whether or not liberty has moral arguments in support of it as an end in itself, it certainly is a necessary precondition if men are to progress efficiently toward the fulfillment of their objectives. On libertarian precepts, tolerance is advocated because no one can be sure that dissenters are not "right," and because, even if they are "wrong," they can gain moral worth only by accepting responsibility for the decisions. From consideration of the conditions for progress, we can say that tolerance will enable a society safely to gain information about which social proposals do or do not enable objectives to be more adequately satisfied.

The role of an experimental group in social innovation is the methodological equivalent of a "limited marketing sample" in business activity. Rather than commit the whole of his resources to a new conjecture, the prudent businessman will market it under test conditions in a limited area. If the results are satisfactory, he will be able to repeat the innovation on a large scale with some assurance of success. If the limited experiment does not succeed, then he will be warned, without too much loss, against an expensive repetition. Tolerance enables society to observe limited marketing samples of social innovations. Only if the new ideas succeed for those who willingly put them to test need the rest of the society think seriously about their adoption; if the experimental groups achieve adverse results, then the rest of society knows one more range of social conjectures to avoid.

There are, of course, problems associated with the expansion of a small-scale adoption to society generally. It might be that what works for a few will not work for many, or that success is dependent upon factors which vary from person to person. As an example from our own times, we might inspect the so-called counterculture. The social innovation it makes for greater fulfillment of aims if one "drops out," drawing welfare payments instead of working for a living, is obviously not susceptible of widespread adoption. Its viability as an alternative requires that there be large numbers who do not adopt it, but continue, instead, to provide the economic resources whereby the welfare payments can be made. The "counterculture" also seems to propose that the conventional culture should be drawn on for such things as medical services and transport, and again carries the implication that it is only an available alternative if it is not widely adopted. It would be more appropriate to refer to it as a "parasitic subculture" rather than a genuine counterculture.

Herbert Marcuse, in his *Critique of Pure Tolerance*,[4] has pointed out some of the harm which might be caused by liberty and tolerance. He says that very often liberty can mean simply the freedom to propagate error, and that liberty must be checked in order that error might be controlled. "Tolerance," he says, "is repressive." It is undoubtedly true that liberty can be a means for the propagation of error; it is also true, however, that it provides the basis for the detection of error. It is not (as Milton implied) that truth will always triumph over error[5] if it competes on equal terms, but rather that liberty will allow counterclaims to be tested, in order that a comparative assessment may be made. If people are free, they may indeed embrace error, but they may also reject it. If they are not free, then they have no choice at all to embrace or to reject what is enforced, nor any means of ascertaining whether or not it *is* error. Marcuse would have us restrict tolerance to the extent required for the elimination of error. The question "But who is to determine what is error and what should be restricted?" is purely rhetorical, since the answer is obvious. Marcuse himself, and those of like mind, will perform for us the onerous task of sorting out truth from falsehood.

In order for society to reap the full benefit of testing by experimental groups, freedom of information is required, in addition to the right of dissent. Only through free expression can proposals and test results be communicated. A society which imposes censorship on discussion of alternatives is denying people the assistance of other minds on their problems. People often (as we noted) show great fondness for their own theories; so it may take the work of others to bring out inadequacies and suggest modifications to overcome defects. The transfer of information from one experimenter to others not only saves time (which might otherwise be wasted in needless repetition of work), it allows full play to the fertility of conjectures by presenting work to as many minds as possible. Rare, indeed, is the problem which cannot be solved more rapidly and more effectively by the application of many minds rather than one. Edmund Burke said he had "never yet seen any plan which has not been mended by the observations of those who were much inferior in understanding to the person who took the lead in the business."[6]

In talking of ease of communication as a necessary constituent of efficient progress, we are talking of two factors. There is the facility of information transfer brought about by technical means and accomplishments. Radio and telephones play their part in this, as do Royal Societies and the publishing industry. That part we have already considered, namely, the ease of communication which comes by the prevalence of free speech and discussion, is the other aspect of the efficient dissemination of information.

But even in a society which protects the free transfer of information there are concealed impediments to full communication of ideas. Limits are imposed by those who control the sources of dissemination. The information transmitted by magazines, newspapers, and radio or television stations depends to some extent upon what the controllers regard as worthy of dissemination. There might be commercial factors at work, too, and reluctance by information media to circulate stories which might offend advertisers. Clearly, diffusion of ownership and control of the agencies which disseminate information will militate in favor of free exchange of news and ideas. Just as competition between producers and sellers guarantees the consumer against the evils of economic monopoly, the diversity of control of communications media serves to protect society against the evils of information monopoly.

Trial and Error

Freedom of criticism and research are obvious necessities. There is little point in allowing free access of information if people are not then free to speculate upon it and to test their speculations. If a political authority is to license research, deciding what is, or is not, a fit subject of inquiry, then progress will be restricted to narrow and artificial channels. Progress is made by testing and rejecting alternative proposals. If this is arbitrarily restricted, not only will men be unable to eliminate inadequacies in certain fields but they will be denied the unimaginable "fallout" from each prohibited line of inquiry.

If progress is to be made, there must be no "infallible" authorities in society. If it is held that some person, book, or creed is without the possibility of error (or can never be improved upon), then capacity to learn from mistakes will be severely restricted. Not only will it be difficult to make conjectures which run counter to the "infallible word," but the latter might also be used as a standard to check theories against, replacing the world of observation. Thus possibly inadequate theories may be retained, and useful ones might be discarded. And if the world of observation is used to evaluate proposals not dealt with by the "infallible word," there will be the attendant difficulties of attempting to reconcile two sets of information, derived from fundamentally different premises, into a coherent body of knowledge.

The men who make progress are those who do *not* think they know all the answers. If people hold the belief that they are in possession of a formula whereby further knowledge may be deduced from existing knowledge, then the range of proposals and the likelihood of testing are both diminished.

When men thought that Aristotle had said all there was to be said about science, there was little stimulus to research. When they thought that inspection of his texts was the surest way to scientific knowledge, they were not inclined to make their own conjectures. When people thought that if observation appeared to run counter to Aristotle's teachings, then the observation must be at fault, there was little scope for improving on Aristotle's proposals. One need only recall that humans who were not in possession of what Aristotle said was the correct number of teeth were written off as "defective specimens" to appreciate how difficult progress becomes in the presence of "infallible" authorities.

There are human societies which claim to be in possession of infallible social doctrines and which restrict experiment with alternatives on the ground that they are less satisfactory. This notion of "less satisfactory" is obtained not from observation of performance in practice but from calculations which derive from the "infallible" authority. These societies are thus deprived of a range of proposals and tests which might reveal alternatives found superior in practice (i.e., *actually* superior) to the "infallible" guide. But even in societies which enforce no obedience to allegedly infallible sources, there are many who make personal obeisance to such sources, and who deliberately seek to confuse or blur the conflicting evidence of practical tests which might run counter to them. The first attempt is to prevent evidence from arising at all; the second is to prevent it from being appreciated for what it is when it cannot be avoided.

It is a common syndrome among those who work from "infallible" sources to insist that *everyone* must be made to follow the proposed plan.[7] They are not content to have the proposed innovation practiced by a few members of society, so that its practical results might be inspected before others commit themselves to it. On the contrary, a clause is usually found somewhere near the center of the grand design to the effect that the plan will not work unless everyone adopts it simultaneously. It does not take an exceptionally suspicious mind to reflect that if no other practice is permitted, it will be very difficult to compare the effects of the innovation with what might have been achieved by alternatives.

By destroying all counterexamples, one is guaranteed at least that the plan will not come out unfavorably from a comparison with alternatives. If no one is allowed access to an objective assessment of its merits, then no one will be able to shake faith in the "infallible" principles which gave rise to it. Those who wish genuine progress to be made, and recognized as such, will always act like scientists in preserving the control group. Small-scale trials, like small-scale marketing, allow results of alternative systems to be compared. Much more to the point, they allow unsuccessful experiments to be written off with no greater loss to society than the damage done to the small group under test. With the universal-scale planners, "infallible" or no, it may be society which has to be written off.

As important as the preservation of alternatives for a basis of comparison is the acceptance of evidence from them. It was observed how it comes about in the world of scientific activity that the originators of theories sometimes cling to them long after evidence from testing has led most scientists to reject them as inadequate. This effect seems even more marked in social and political activity, where simple belief is reinforced by ideological commitment. The student who remarked "In science, if the evidence conflicts with the theory, one rejects the theory; in the social sciences one rejects the evidence!" was certainly exaggerating.[8] Yet the tenacity with which theories are retained in spite of conflicting evidence seems much more marked in that activity than in the more austere discipline of science. Professor Peter Bauer pointed to the heart of the problem by explaining that "when a proposition is held as an article of faith, the evidence becomes irrelevant."[9]

Professor Bauer's thesis[10] affords a good example of treatment of the evidence. His claims concerning the efficiency of overseas development aid are both contentious and controversial. Whether he is correct or incorrect in his assertion that overseas development aid is useless as a promoter of growth, and actually does the recipient country more harm than good, can hardly be considered in any detail herein; but his comments on the way evidence is received are highly relevant. His claim is that because the proponents of overseas development aid are committed to a *belief* in its efficiency, then evidence of economic growth by the recipient is taken as proof that it works, whereas evidence of lack of growth is taken as proof that more aid is needed. The "aid brigade" wins every time, whether the coin falls heads or tails. If, instead of being held as an article of faith, the view concerning the efficiency of aid were advanced as a scientific-type proposition, with its retention or rejection depending upon the results of trials, Bauer claims that the evidence would have led us to discard it. Whether or not he is correct in this assertion, he is certainly right to point out that, with current treatment of the evidence, the claim concerning the efficiency of aid in stimulating growth is not put at risk in any trial whatsoever—that no event could occur that might lead us to its modification or rejection.

If a proposition is held as an article of faith in such a way that no evidence could conceivably lead to its change or abandonment, then, insofar as it operates within our two-part formula of progress, it differs in no wise from an untestable proposition. If the evidence is indeed irrelevant, then the proposition cannot be tested comparatively against rival or counter propositions, and it cannot, therefore, be of any assistance toward progress. When the evidence is ignored or rejected out of a desire to retain the theory, we are no longer engaged in the activity of social progress.[11]

Not only is it important that the evidence of the results of proposals be available for inspection unrestricted and unconfused, it is vital that there should be the capability of evaluating alternative achievement levels, and of criticizing prevailing practices. The formal freedom to criticize will be of no value to progress unless it is accompanied by conditions calculated to inculcate the propensity to exercise critical faculties. A society which has no concept of alternatives, either

Trial and Error

of achievements or of practices, will not engage in criticism of its own ways. It is the spectacle of different ways of doing things which leads to criticism and innovation.

The dictum of the eighteenth-century rationalists that "knowledge is freedom" expresses the simple truism that choice cannot be made in the absence of alternatives. While freedom to select between available choices without the arbitrary imposition of another's will should not be confused with extensions to the range of choices available,[12] it is correct to recognize that freedom can only be exercised through choice, and is valueless without it. The more choices there are available, the more valuable freedom becomes. The eighteenth-century rationalists recognized that knowledge brings awareness of available alternatives, and can thus put substance into the empty shell of formal freedom.

When a society is uniform, and insulated from external contact, its ways of doing things are seen as *the* ways of doing things, not as one group of practices among many alternatives. The traditions of an insulated society are not seen as chosen alternatives but as necessary practices. It takes contrast with other ways for existing ways to be *recognized* as ways. Inhabitants of an island do not recognize it as an island until they have seen other islands: it takes two of an object before one of them requires a name. In a universe consisting of naught but blue spheres, there would be no notion of blueness or sphericity; only with the introduction of something like a red cube would there come the recognition that everything else was blue and spherical, as well as merely "there."[13]

The lack of progress in sheltered societies "happens" partly because of the lack of external examples of attainment, partly through lack of appreciation that there could be alternatives. The typical insulated society is not marked by progress, but by the rule of tribal law, ritual, and taboo. Only when the members of such a society come into contact with members of alternative cultures do they begin to appreciate that what they thought of as inevitable ways were only viable alternatives. Quite possibly the initial reaction to such an encounter might be marked by disgust and horror at the apparently "unnatural" practices engaged in by other societies, but there follows the realization that other societies seem to achieve what they regard as adequate results by alternative practices. Inevitably there comes comparison. Even if the man exposed to other-culture contact for the first time opts for his own ways, the decision is now a conscious one, not an unthinking acceptance. What had been accepted as natural and inevitable now begins to be evaluated in terms of the ends achieved. People begin to think in terms of incorporating practices from other societies in order to improve their own, and criticism is born.

The stages by which an isolated society is transformed by cultural contact into a critical and improving one can be described by the psychological steps which are taken. Contact leads to appreciation of alternatives; consideration of alternatives leads to comparison; comparison leads to evaluation; evaluation to criticism; criticism to improvement. It is but a short step from the consideration of actual alternatives to the postulation of hypothetical ones, from proposing the adoption of practices which prevail elsewhere to the suggestion of practices which exist only in the imagination. The step from emulation to innovation is short for minds equipped to take it; and it is from the cross-fertilization of cultures in contact that we can expect the development of such minds. The awareness of alternatives is a vital ingredient for development of the critical and creative mentality. It is a prerequisite of progress.

Any consideration of the optimum conditions which can be applied to assist the development of progress must therefore take account of the value of cultural contact with other societies. Where there is the ability, both technical and legal, to visit alien cultures, to receive visitors from them, to read about other societies and to investigate aspects concerning them, there will be prevailing circumstances of the type which must be present if criticism and inventive proposal are to be promoted.

An inspection of human history with this in mind shows that societies which have made further and faster progress toward fulfillment of the aims of their citizens have been those which were placed in circumstances of expanded contact with other cultures. Every spurt of human achievement which has been found dramatic enough to be given the name of a "renaissance" or "enlightenment" can be traced back to the point at which a comparatively insulated society suddenly found itself in sustained and far-reaching contact with other cultures. It is the Athenians, with their shipborne cultural frontier, whom we remember for their progress—not the Spartans, with their isolated and tribalistic society. It is the Italians, with their merchant princes, whom we remember for the beginnings of the Renaissance in Europe. It is the English, with their ships, who produced the cultural advances of the first Elizabethan age. It is the Scots, suddenly dragged from comparative isolation by the union with England, who made such leaps within a single generation that the term *Scottish Enlightenment* was coined to describe the proliferation of genius.

It would appear that we are witnessing one of the general (and testable) sociohistorical laws referred to in chapter 5. It seems reasonable to propose that progress is made dramatically by those societies which change from a relatively isolated position to one in which they have greatly increased access to other cultures. Just as the American historian Frederick Jackson Turner[14] proposed that it was contact with the frontier which led European settlers to adopt the salient characteristics of an American culture,[15] we propose that there is a psychological equivalent of the American frontier in circumstances of sudden cultural contact. This "cultural frontier" implies the appreciation of alternatives, the comparison, evaluation, criticism, and creative imagination which are the hallmarks of a progressing society. Whereas the American frontier bred self-reliance, social egalitarianism, respect for democratic values, and an easy class mobility, the cultural frontier breeds critical, innovating, and decision-making man. These are the very characteristics required for the successful and efficient operation of the formula of progress.

It is evident, then, that society can exert conscious control over such an intangible phenomenon as the creative imagination. Without fully understanding its source, there can be appreciation of the conditions under which it arises, and deliberate action to institute and maintain those conditions. These conditions include wide access to the practices and ideas of other societies, and a free exchange of information with them. It is a kind of pluralism of the international community. Until now, we have been concerned with societies, and with groups and individuals in societies. But the whole human race may be considered a kind of society, with individual nations and cultures making up the groups within it.

What we found to be true for an individual society with its internal experimenting groups need be no less true for the international community of man. We can say of that community, as we said of an individual society, that progress will be made if there is variety in its practices and free passage of information among the different groups. The conditions required for progress on the small scale apply no less on the world scale. Nations and cultures may emulate successful examples elsewhere, just as individuals and groups may copy successful innovators within a society; and the same freedoms are required if the process is to operate efficiently. The more these conditions prevail over the international community of nations, the more does each individual culture stand to gain from its contact with the others. It has been argued that world peace is unlikely until more uniform institutions and practices are established under a world government. This may be true, but we should remember the other side of the coin, and appreciate that it is the very diversity of alternative and competing cultural practices which provides such an important ingredient of progress toward achievement of human ends.

This inspection of the conditions appropriate to the most efficient operation of the equation of progress leads us, finally, to postulate what sort of society will constitute the optimum society for progress. It will be, first and foremost, what can be called a "free" society. Its legal framework and institutions must be such that there is freedom to evaluate, to criticize, to comment upon the value of established practices. There must be freedom, too, to propose alternatives, to speculate on possible improvements. A large measure of liberty must necessarily be granted those who would wish to innovate in social behavior, to experiment with proposed lifestyles. It must be a tolerant society, as well as formally free, since social pressures can be as effective as legal interdicts in prohibiting the testing of alternatives. It probably follows from this that it must be a stable society, even if the stability derives from a commitment to gradual improvement. From our observations concerning the role of custom and tradition, it may be seen that tolerance comes more readily from a society which does not feel threatened. Almost certainly it must be a democratic society, meaning there must at least be provision for the peaceful replacement of the ruling group from time to time, even if it is not one in which the "will of the people" prevails in political life.

Above all, such a society would be characterized by its pluralism and its diffusion of power. It would be marked by a variety of social attitudes and practices, being tested simultaneously by different groups, and by the absence of any kind of monopoly control over the dissemination of information. Putting this in political language, we might talk in terms of a free press and publishing industry, with widespread and diverse control over communications media. Contact with other cultures would be relatively unrestricted, and its citizens free to travel abroad, to receive visitors from abroad, and to read foreign material and listen to foreign radio stations. We are talking about a society which has at least some characteristics of the "democracy" so castigated by Plato, in his ranking of states in their various phases of degeneration.[16] But from the point of view of progress toward the fulfillment of man's aims, this society is considerably more attractive than Plato's alternatives.

The state of the "optimum society for progress" can be summarized by saying that it must recognize the value of tested proposals, and make its decisions on the basis of test results. Then there will always be preserved the grounds for comparison of alternative proposals, and the grounds for making decisions on the basis of that comparison.

Notes

[1] This is an idea developed from J. S. Mill by F. A. von Hayek, though its roots are older, as the quotation from Milton shows. Hayek quotes F. Schiller (*On the Aesthetic Education of Man*) as saying "Man must have his freedom to be ready for morality."

[2] John Milton, *Areopagitica*.

[3] F. A. von Hayek, *The Constitution of Liberty* (1960).

[4] Herbert Marcuse, R. P. Wolff, and Barrington Moore, *A Critique of Pure Tolerance* (1967).

[5] This is a reference to Milton's *Areopagitica:* "Let her and falsehood grapple; who ever knew truth put to the worse, in a free and open encounter?"

Popper attacks Milton's idea of "manifest" truth in his essay "On the Sources of Knowledge and of Ignorance" (*Conjectures and Refutations* [1963]).

[6] Edmund Burke.

Trial and Error

[7] Popper attacks what he calls "holistic social experiments" in sec. 24 of his *Poverty of Historicism* (1957).

[8] I am indebted to Mr. Atholl D. Robertson for this remark.

[9] A comment made in the BBC "Controversy" television program which featured Professor Bauer in September 1972.

[10] Peter Bauer, *Dissent on Development; Two Views on Overseas Aid; Development Economics: The Spurious Consensus;* and other works.

[11] Nor are we engaged in the acquisition of knowledge.

[12] Hayek discusses the various types of freedoms in his *Constitution of Liberty,* and the point is explored further by Fritz Machlup in his essay "Liberalism and the Choice of Freedoms" (*Roads to Freedom,* edited by Erich Streissler [1969]).

[13] The point (and the example) are from Bernard Mayo's *The Logic of Personality* (1952).

[14] Frederick Jackson Turner, *The Frontier in American History* (1920, but based on essays of the 1890s).

[15] Described by Daniel J. Boorstin in *The Americans—1: The Colonial Experience* (1958).

[16] In Plato's *Republic,* bk. VIII.

Conclusion

In the world of evolution, the instruments of change and development are mutation and selection. Random mutations produce offspring which differ from their parents, and the new individuals are tested by their ability to survive in the prevailing environment. Many die. Many do not even survive the process of birth. But when a change is favorable, the individual which "carries" it survives; and its offspring which "carry" such changes also survive. In a competitive environment, the new strain outperforms its rivals, and survives preferentially to become the new norm of the species.

Evolution is slow by our time scale, not only because the individual's fate is linked to that of the change it carries, but also because the changes are made at random. With complex organisms, dependent on a delicate balance of parts, the chance is very high indeed that any change will be adverse. It may take thousands of generations before the lucky accident of low statistical probability will occur.

The changes made purposefully by man in the pursuit of his objectives occur at a faster rate. In the first place, the survival of the individual who produces the innovation is not linked to the fate of the idea. If the innovation proves inferior and has to be rejected, the same individual can survive to produce other ideas, as well as offspring. The second reason, and the more important of the two, is that man's changes are not made at random. They are backed by the inspiration of a creative imagination. Man's innovations are purposefully directed toward the satisfaction of his aims. They are not produced haphazardly, as some accident of the night, but are the product of a thinking mind, a mind which can reject many possible alternatives without even the need to formulate them explicitly. The ideas which man produces are those which he thinks will work, will succeed in bringing him what he wants.

The survival of man's inspirations, like the survival of mutated offspring, depends upon their ability to outperform their rivals. Here, too, the advantage lies with man. He can use his creative imagination to bring competing ideas rapidly to a point of crisis, at which the superiority of one of them will be shown, and this will enable inferior rivals to be rejected. The basis of that superiority is, as I have shown, the capacity for innovation to assist man to gain his chosen objectives.

Unlucky accidents, as well as lucky ones, occur in the evolutionary process. A favorable mutation might be destroyed by some freak act of misfortune before it can pass on its innovation. The mutated individual might be struck by lightning or killed by a falling tree before it can breed, and it might be thousands of generations, if at all, before the lucky accident recurs. With man's ideas, however, there is always the possibility of rehabilitation. An innovation that is rejected at the time of its formulation survives its creator, and continues to be available to other men who might wish to test it again if circumstances change in the future.

In his attempts to achieve his aims, man makes use of a method which bears similarity in its logical elements to the methods of evolution. It is a superior method because it has the inspired mind of man behind it. This distinction provides the basis for our assurance that the changes which man is

Trial and Error

making for himself have far outstripped the changes which are being made by evolution. Man's propensity to seek control over his circumstances has given him the instrument to outstrip nature even in his own development. His method of change is faster because his mind is involved in it.

If man, by analysis of the method by which he makes progress, comes to understand the conditions under which progress can operate, he gives himself the choice of allowing those conditions to prevail. In which case, by extending the range of decisions available for men to make, this book will have made a modest contribution to human achievement.

Bibliography

Appley, M. H. *See* Cofer, C. N.
Ardrey, Robert. *The Social Contract: A Personal Inquiry into the Evolutionary Source of Order and Disorder.* New York: Atheneum, 1970.
―――. *The Territorial Imperative: A Personal Inquiry into the Animal Origins of Property and Nations.* New York: Atheneum, 1966.
Bauer, Peter. *Dissent on Development: Studies and Debates in Development Economics.* Cambridge, Mass.: Harvard University Press, 1972.
Bauer, Peter, and Ward, Barbara. *Two Views on Aid to Underdeveloped Countries.* Institute of Economic Affairs Occasional Papers, no. 9, 1966.
Bauer, Peter, and Yamey, B. S. *The Economics of Underdeveloped Countries.* Cambridge: At the University Press, 1967.
Beichman, Arnold. *Nine Lies About America.* La Salle, Ill.: Open Court, Library Press, 1972.
Blake, Robert. *The Conservative Party from Peel to Churchill.* London: Eyre & Spottiswoode, 1970. New York: St Martin's Press, 1971.
Boorstin, Daniel J. *The Americans.* Vol. 1: *The Colonial Experience.* New York: Random House, 1958.

Burke, Edmund. *Reflections on the Revolution in France.* 1790. Modern edition, edited by Conor Cruise O'Brien. New York: Penguin, 1976.
Bury, J. B. *The Idea of Progress.* London: Macmillan, 1920.
Carnap, Rudolf. *Philosophy and Logical Syntax.* London: Routledge & Kegan Paul, 1935.
Carr, E. H. *What Is History?* New York: St Martin's Press, 1961.
Cecil, Lord Hugh. *Conservatism.* London: Williams & Northgate, 1912.
Cofer, C. N., and Appley, M. H. *Motivation: Theory and Research.* New York: Wiley, 1964.
Eysenck, H. J. *The IQ Argument: Race, Intelligence and Education.* La Salle, Ill.: Open Court, Library Press, 1971.
Fisher, H. A. L. *History of Europe.* London: Eyre & Spottiswoode, 1935.
Fitts, Paul M., and Posner, Michael I. *Human Performance.* Basic Concepts in Psychology Series. Belmont, Calif.: Brooks/Cole, 1967.
Friedman, Milton. *Capitalism and Freedom.* Chicago: University of Chicago Press, 1962.
Galbraith, J. K. *American Capitalism.* Boston: Houghton Mifflin, 1952.
──────. *Economic Development.* Cambridge, Mass.: Harvard University Press, 1964.
Hart, H. L. A. *Law, Liberty and Morality.* Stanford: Stanford University Press, 1963.
Hayek, Friedrich A. von. *The Constitution of Liberty.* Chicago: University of Chicago Press, 1960.
──────. *The Road to Serfdom.* Chicago: University of Chicago Press; London: Routledge & Kegan Paul, 1944.
──────. *Studies in Philosophy, Politics and Economics.* Chicago: University of Chicago Press, 1967.
──────. "The Use of Knowledge in Society." *American Economic Review* 35 (1945).
Helson, H. *Adaptation-Level Theory.* New York: Harper & Row, 1964.
Huxley, Aldous. *Brave New World.* New York: Harper & Row, 1932.

Jensen, A. R., et al. *Environment, Heredity and Intelligence.* Harvard Reprint Series, no. 2. Cambridge, Mass.: Harvard University Press, 1969.

Kuhn, Thomas S. "Reflections on My Critics." In *Criticism and the Growth of Knowledge,* edited by Imre Lakatos and Alan Musgrave. Cambridge: At the University Press, 1970.

———. *The Structure of Scientific Revolutions.* Chicago: University of Chicago Press, 1962

Lakatos, Imre. "Falsification and the Methodology of Scientific Research Programmes." In *Criticism and the Growth of Knowledge,* edited by Imre Lakatos and Alan Musgrave. Cambridge: At the University Press, 1970.

Lorenz, Konrad. *King Solomon's Ring.* New York: Crowell, 1952.

———. *On Aggression.* London: Methuen, 1963.

Mace, C. A. "Homeostasis, Needs and Values." *British Journal of Psychology,* 1953.

Machlup, Fritz. "Liberalism and the Choice of Freedoms." In *Roads to Freedom: Essays in Honor of Friedrich A. von Hayek,* edited by Erich Streissler. London: Routledge & Kegan Paul; Clifton, N. J.: Augustus Kelley, 1969.

MacIntyre, Alasdair. *Marcuse.* London: Fontana (Collins), 1970.

Marcuse, Herbert; Wolff, R. P.; and Moore, Barrington. *A Critique of Pure Tolerance.* London: Cape, 1969.

Mayo, Bernard. *The Logic of Personality.* London: Cape, 1952.

Mill, John Stuart. *On Liberty.*

———. *Utilitarianism.*

Musgrave, Alan. *See* Lakatos, Imre.

Oakeshott, Michael. *Rationalism in Politics and Other Essays.* London: Methuen, 1962.

Packard, Vance. *The Hidden Persuaders.* New York: McKay, 1957.

Plumb, J. H. "The Historian's Dilemma." 1964.

Pollard, Sidney. *The Idea of Progress.* New York: Basic Books, 1968.

Popper, Sir Karl. *Conjectures and Refutations.* New York: Basic Books, 1962.

———. "Indeterminism Is Not Enough." *Encounter,* April 1973, pp. 20–26.

———. *The Logic of Scientific Discovery.* Originally published as

Logik der Forschung, 1934. English version. New York: Basic Books, 1959.

⸺. *The Open Society and Its Enemies.* London: Routledge & Kegan Paul, 1945.

⸺. *The Poverty of Historicism.* First published in 1944–45. Reprinted in book form. Boston: Beacon Press, 1957.

Posner, Michael I. *See* Fitts, Paul M.

Quine, Willard Van Orman. *From a Logical Point of View.* Cambridge, Mass.: Harvard University Press, 1953

Rostow, W. W. *The Stages of Economic Growth.* Cambridge: At the University Press, 1960.

Rundle, Bede. "Anglo-Saxon Approaches." *Encounter,* November 1973, pp. 67–73.

Ryle, Gilbert. *The Concept of Mind.* New York: Barnes & Noble, 1949.

Sakoff, A. N. "The Private Sector in Soviet Agriculture." In the monthly bulletin of *Agricultural Economics,* FAO, Rome (November 9, 1962).

Skinner, B. F. "The Phylogeny and Ontogeny of Human Behaviour." *Science* 153 (1966): 1205–13.

⸺. *Science and Human Behavior.* New York: Macmillan, 1953.

Smith, Adam. *The Wealth of Nations.*

Smode, A. "Learning and Performance in a Tracking Task under Two Levels of Achievement Information Feedback." *Journal of Experimental Psychology,* 1958.

Stone, Lawrence. *Social Change and Revolution in England, 1540–1640.* Problems and Perspectives in History Series. London: Longmans, 1965.

Tinbergen, Niko. *The Herring Gull's World.* New Naturalist Series. London: Collins, 1953.

Tocqueville, Alexis de. *Democracy in America.*

Turner, Frederick Jackson. *The Frontier in American History.* Originally published as essays in the 1890s. Republished in book form. New York: Holt, 1920. Reprint. Huntington, N. Y.: Kreiger, 1976.

Van Doren, Charles. *The Idea of Progress.* New York: Praeger, 1967.

Walcott, R. R. *English Politics in the Early Eighteenth Century.* Cambridge, Mass.: Harvard University Press, 1956.

Walsh, W. H. *An Introduction to the Philosophy of History.* New York: Hutchinson, 1951.

Index

Adler, Alfred, 65 n.13
advertising, coercive, 138, 155 n.11
aims, comparative, 128; contradictory, 3; conventional, 69–70, 74, 79–80, 105–10, 118, 124, 132, 191, 197, 200, 206; economic, ch. 7; hierarchy of, 8, 112, 123, 169; of members in society, 157, 169–70; social, ch. 6
alienation, 161
Appley, M. H., 76
architecture, 25
aristocracy, 99
Aristotle, 97, 197–98
Armstrong, Neil, 147
art, 71, 97
astronomy, 109
Athenians, 203
athletics, 4
atomic weight, 22–23, 28
augmented feedback, 78–79

background knowledge. *See* knowledge, background
background theory, 29

Bannister, Roger, 76
Bauer, Peter, 199–200
Beeching, Dr., 120 n.1
Beichman, Arnold, 2
belief, 20, 45 n.10, 56–57, 200
Bentham, Jeremy, 123–24
Berkeley, Bishop, 64 n.1
biology, 46 n.16, 94, 100
Blake, Lord, 101 n.3
blink microscope, 109
Booth, General, 154
Brave New World, 13 n.17
Burke, Edmund, 158, 196

calculation, distrust of, 158, 162–64
Carnap, Rudolf, 64 n.1
Carr, E. H., 93, 102 n.13
Cecil, Lord Hugh, 158
censorship, 195
central direction, 137–39, 142–43, 145–47, 151–52. *See also* planning, economic
Chadwick, Sir Edwin, 124
Christians, 9
Cofer, C. N., 76

collective progress, 127
common sense, 15, 19, 50
communication, 195–96, 206
comparative aims, 128
competitive (or comparative) testing, ch. 2 (29–48), 49–62 passim, 81, 85, 91–93, 99–101, 108–9, 112–15, 120, 123, 129, 135–36, 140–47 passim, 174, 176, 191
consistency, 17, 21, 28, 99
consumer satisfaction, 134–36, 146, 150, 152, 155 n.12, 182
contradictory aims, 3
control group, 185
controlled experiment, 92
conventional aim or target, 69–70, 74, 79–80, 105–10, 118, 124, 132, 191, 197, 200, 206
conventionalism, 22, 24, 34, 46 n.12, 54, 64
corpuscular theory of light, 28, 179
correspondence with facts, 15, 18, 52
counterculture, 194–95
covering law theory, 88–89, 91, 100
crisis point (in testing), 30–35, 49, 85, 99–100, 191, 210
crystals, 90
custom, ch. 8, 205

Darwin, Charles, 46 n.16
dating (in history), 99
decay of atoms, 90
degenerating problemshift, 53
demarcation, 49–50, 53, 57, 62–65
democracy, 180–86, 192, 205–6
Democritus, atomic theory of, 57–58
development aid, 199–200
Dickinson, Harry T., 98

discontent, 149, 168, 192
distrust of calculation, 158, 162–64
documentation (in history), 99

economics, 110–12, ch. 7 (128–56), 157, 175, 182, 184, 192
Einstein, Albert, model of observed universe of, versus Newton's, 27
emulation, 115–16, 143, 149, 169–70, 173, 177, 180, 202
engineering, 25
entrepreneurs, 134–35
envy, 149
epistemology, 59, 153
equilibrium price, 129–30
ethology, 160
European culture, 176–78
evolution, 46 n.16, 94, 100, 113, 120, 123, 145, 209–11

fairness, 151–52
falsification, 15–18, 27, 32, 45–46, 50–51, 65 n.3
falsity content, 15–22 passim, 52
falsity, criterion of, 16
familiarity, 158, 169
feedback, 31, 62, 74, 77–79
fertility of theories, 62, 147, 196
Fisher, H. A. L., 101 n.5
Fitts, Paul M., 75, 79
foreign (or external) example, 172–73, 192, 201–3
Frankenstein, 13
frontier hypothesis, 203–4
future knowledge. *See* knowledge, future

Galbraith, John Kenneth, 155 n.11, 188 n.16
Gaussian curve, 95–96, 103 n.14

geology, 87–88, 94, 99
Gibbon, Edward, 97
gossip, 86–87

handicrafts, 125–26
Hart, H. L. A., 178
Hayek, Friedrich A. von, 90, 155 n.17, 178, 206 n.1, 207 n.12
Helson, H., 75
Hempel, Carl, 88
hierarchy of aims, 8, 112, 123, 169
history, 8, ch. 5
Hobbes, Thomas, 64 n.1
Holmes, Geoffrey S., 98
human performance, 72, 75–76, 112
Hume, David, 20, 64 n.1

identity, drive for, 113, 162, 166
inconsistency, 17, 19, 27
index (in historical study), 91
induction, 5–6, 20, 38, 162
Industrial Revolution, 4
infallibility, 197–98
initial conditions, 88, 91, 93, 100
innovators, 76, 116, 134–36, 168, 176, 180, 185, 194, 202, 205, 209–10
intelligence quotient, 96
investment, 134
Italians, 203

knowledge, application of, "how" versus "that," 8, 67; background, 17, 22–23; future, 115; objective, 16, 18, 45; practical, 68–69, 71–74, 82; technical, 68–69, 71–74, 81, 115
Kuhn, Thomas S., 5, 10, 23, 38–44, 47 n.21 and n.24, 108

laissez-faire, 137, 155 n.10
Lakatos, Imre, 16–17, 22–24, 46 n.12
laws of history, 88–101, 102 n.8
liberty, 119, 178, 193, 197, 200–201, 205
literature, history as, 97
logical positivism, 49–51
Lorenz, Konrad, 159
Lysenko, T. D., 38

McDonagh, Oliver, thesis of, 154
Mace, C. A., 76
Machlup, Fritz, 207 n.12
Manhattan Project, 144
Marcuse, Herbert, 195
market economy, 132–55, 184
market mechanisms, 129–30
Marx, Karl, theories of, 66
Masai, 161
meaningfulness, standards of, 49–51
mercantilists, 154
metaphysical propositions, ch. 3, 67
Methodism, 179
Mill, John Stuart, 119, 176–79
Milton, John, 193, 195, 206 n.5
models, 7, 20–43, 75, 108, 131, 141, 184
monopoly, 137, 155 n.10, 173, 196, 205
motivation (motives), 38, 79–80, 192; economic, ch. 7; social, ch. 6
Muggeridge, Malcolm, 181

Newton, Sir Isaac, 27, 29, 46 n.16. *See also* Einstein, Albert.
nonconclusive arguments, 6
nonscience, 51, 53, 65 n.3

Oakeshott, Michael, 67–82 passim, 82 n.7, 161, 187 n.12
objective knowledge. *See* knowledge, objective
objectivism, 24
optimism, 11

Packard, Vance, 155 n.11
paradigm, scientific, 39–42, 44
pattern generalizations, 90
planning, economic, 140–48, 152. *See also* central direction
Plato, 206
Plumb, J. H., 1, 3
pluralism in society, 174–79, 183–84, 204–5
Pollard, Sidney, 188 n.16
Popper, Sir Karl R., 5–6, 15–16, 22–43 passim, 45 n.10, 47 n.17, 50–54, 62, 64 n.1, 65 n.3 and n.5, 66 n.15, 88–89, 121 n.8, 184, 187 n.11, 188 n.19, 206 n.5, 207 n.7
Posner, Michael I., 75, 79
practical knowledge. *See* knowledge, practical
preconceived theory, 29
prediction, 24–37, 52, 58, 60–61, 80, 90–94, 112, 131–35, 141–42, 179, 192; self-fulfilling, in planned economies, 142, in social science, 102 n.11; self-negating, in social science, 102 n.11
price mechanism, 138, 153
probability, 94–96
production bonus, 145
progressive problemshift, 53
progressive taxation, 150
Prout, William 22–23, 28

quantum theory, 28, 179

rationing, 154
realism, 15–17
religion, 60, 80
retrodiction, 24–28, 65 n.10, 92–94, 97–98, 100
Rise of the Gentry issue, 99
ritual, 201
Romans, 9
Rostow, W. W., 11, 13 n.19
Royal Society, 196
Rundle, Bede, 64 n.2
Ryle, Gilbert, 67

sanctions against experiment, 171–73, 205
Schiller, Friedrich, 206
science and scientific activity (method), 4–8, 10, 12, ch. 2, 50–55, 57, 59, 63, 75, 87, 90–94, 97–100, 105, 108, 111–12, 117, 119, 131, 134–35, 141, 176–77, 185, 192, 199
Scottish Enlightenment, 203
security, drive for, 113, 162; in society, 116, 131, 136, 138
self-fulfilling predictions, in planned economies, 142; in social science, 102 n.11
self-love, 160–62
self-negating predictions, in social science, 102 n.11
senses, deception of, 17, 32, 50, 98
skills, 8, ch. 4, 105, 115, 143
slavery, 111, 175
Smith, Adam, 148
Smode, A., 78–79
social sciences, 8, 85–86, 101 n.2, 102 n.11, 123; unification of, 46 n.16
social scientists, 61, 88, 177, 186
sociohistorical laws, 88–101, 102 n.8, 203

Soviet agriculture, 144–45
space research, 148
Spartans, 203
Speck, William A., 98
stimulation, drive for, 113
survival, 113, 160, 178, 209–10
suspicion of the unknown, 158

taboo, 201
Tarski, Alfred, 15
technical knowledge. *See* knowledge, technical
technology and technological advances, 10, 13 n.17, 57, 134, 142, 175
territory, 159–61
theory, atomic, of Democritus, 57–58; background, 29; corpuscular, of light, 28, 179; covering law, 88–89, 91, 100; fertility of, 62, 147, 196; of Karl Marx, 66; of truth, 15; preconceived, 29; quantum 28, 179; wave, of light, 28, 179
tolerance, 179, 193–95, 205
trade unions, 155 n.13
tradition, ch. 8, 201, 205
tribal law, 201
truth content, 16, 22, 52, 65 n.6
truth, theory of, 15
Turner, Frederick Jackson, 203

untestable propositions, 8, ch. 3, 98, 200
usefulness, 55, 57–60, 64
utilitarianism, 119, 123–24, 127, 154 n.5

verification, 50, 60, 64 n.2
verisimilitude, 15–18, 22, 52
Vienna Circle, 49–50, 64 n.1

Walcott, R. R., 98–99
Walsh, W. H., 85
waste, economic, 139–41
wave theory of light, 28, 179
Wittgenstein, Ludwig, 64 n.1
world government, 204
"World III," 42–43, 187 n.11

¢/HG   R/S3LBT
WW #3000 PIRIE